Ray Bradbury and the
Poetics of Reverie
Fantasy, Science Fiction, and the Reader

Studies in Speculative Fiction, No. 2

Robert Scholes, Series Editor

Alumni/Alumnae Professor of English
Brown University

Other Titles in This Series

Ray Bradbury and the Poetics of Reverie
Fantasy, Science Fiction, and the Reader

by
William F. Touponce

UMI RESEARCH PRESS
Ann Arbor, Michigan

Produced and distributed by
UMI Research Press
an imprint of
University Microfilms International
A Xerox Information Resources Company
Ann Arbor, Michigan 48106

Library of Congress Cataloging in Publication Data

Touponce, William F.
Ray Bradbury and the poetics of reverie.

(Studies in speculative fiction ; no. 2)
Revision of thesis — University of Massachusetts,
1981.
Bibliography: p.
Includes index.
1. Bradbury, Ray, 1920-   —Criticism and interpre-
tation. 2. Fantastic fiction, American—History and
criticism. 3. Science fiction, American—History and
criticism. 4. Reader-response criticism. I. Title.
II. Series.
PS3503.R167Z88 1984   813'.54   84-2553
ISBN 0-8357-1569-8

For Dorothy

Je suis seul, donc nous sommes quatre
Gaston Bachelard

Contents

Acknowledgments

An earlier version of chapter 5 first appeared in *Other Worlds: Fantasy And Science Fiction Since 1939,* edited by John J. Teunissen, with a preface by Ray Bradbury (MOSAIC, 1980), pp. 203-218.

Quotations from Gaston Bachelard *On Poetic Imagination and Reverie,* translated by Colette Gaudin, are reprinted by permission of Bobbs-Merrill Company, copyright © 1971.

Quotations from Gaston Bachelard *The Poetics of Space,* translated by Maria Jolas, copyright © 1958 by Presses Universitaires de France, translation copyright © 1964 by the Orion Press, and from Gaston Bachelard *The Poetics of Reverie,* translated by Daniel Russell, copyright © 1960 by Presses Universitaires de France, translation copyright © 1969 by Grossman Publishers, are reprinted by permission of Viking Penguin Inc.

Quotations from J. R. R. Tolkien *The Tolkien Reader,* copyright © 1966 by J. R. R. Tolkien, are reprinted by permission of Houghton Mifflin Company.

Unless otherwise mentioned, all other translations are my own. Full information concerning all references included in the text will be found in the bibliography.

Quotations from *The Golden Apples of the Sun,* © copyright 1953 by Ray Bradbury, renewed 1981 by Ray Bradbury, from "Cistern," 1947 by Ray Bradbury, renewed 1974, and *Fahrenheit 451,* 1953 by Ray Bradbury, renewed 1981 by Ray Bradbury, are reprinted by permission of Don Congdon Associates, Inc. Quotations from "The Sea Shell," are reprinted by permission of Ray Bradbury. I am grateful to the author for permission to reprint.

I am grateful to the editors and publishers for permission to reprint.

Introduction

This study attempts to provide a phenomenological account of the reader's response to fantasy and science-fiction literature written by the American fantasist, Ray Bradbury (b.1920). Why phenomenological? And why Bradbury? For a number of interrelated reasons.

First of all, because when we respond to the aesthetic experience of fantasy or science fiction, we are reacting to a concrete vibrant world which we have in fact helped to create. We do not respond simply to a collection of formalist devices or a hierarchy of linguistic structures. Most readers of fantasy and science fiction seem to recognize intuitively their sub-creative (to borrow a word coined by J. R. R. Tolkien) roles. And most readers of Bradbury's fantasy recognize its potential for oblique social criticism.[1] Yet in recent theoretical accounts of fantasy literature (I will deal with science fiction separately below) this complex experience of the reader tends to lose its relationship to historical content. The reader has been reduced to a mere passive adjunct of genre theory.

Two examples of this tendency immediately come to mind. Tzvetan Todorov's *The Fantastic* (1970) transforms language into the content of the fantastic. The fantastic in this study, which is largely confined to the nineteenth century, is a kind of rhetorical discourse, and the reader's role consists in following the numerous indications given by the process of utterance *(énonciation)* as they are presented within the text itself.[2] Apart from identifying with a character, all this linguistic reader is required to do is to doubt or hesitate about the nature of a supernatural event, which in the last analysis is reduced to language anyway: "If the fantastic constantly makes use of rhetorical figures, it is because it originates in them. The supernatural is born of language, it is both its consequence and its proof. . .language alone enables us to conceive what is always absent: the supernatural."[3]

The second example is Eric S. Rabkin's *The Fantastic in Literature* (1976), a study which transforms content into form by arguing that the more a text lays bare its devices, the more fantastic it is (and Rabkin's example of pure fantasy is Lewis Carroll's *Alice in Wonderland)*. In the chapter on the fantastic and literary history, for instance, Rabkin argues that "if one cannot exaggerate content, then one must exaggerate form. After World War II, driven to more fantastic writing, the detective tale became more self-reflexive, more concerned with its own ontology as fiction.''[4] Apparently, it was only the wearing out of conventions within the genre which "drove" writers to make these changes, for no direct linkages between literature and society are specified by Rabkin. In any case, the reader's role is reduced in this formalist study almost as starkly as it is in Todorov's structuralist study. It consists in interpreting certain stylistic signals indicating the presence of the fantastic with reference to narrative ground rules, and mainly in the effect of astonishment when these rules are suddenly subverted.

A crucial concept missing in both these studies, although it is indeed often nominally present, is that of world. In this study I plan to show that only a phenomenological account is capable of treating adequately the irreducible nature of fantastic worlds by describing precisely how such worlds are built up in the reading process. Since phenomenology is the philosophy of life-worlds, it is ideally suited to such a task. Its very techniques and methods are designed not to be reductive, but rather to uncover the network of hidden intentional processes by which we inhabit the horizons of the world. Furthermore, as early as 1931, with the publication in German of Roman Ingarden's *The Literary Work of Art,* phenomenological aestheticians were investigating the ways in which the text holds in readiness a world for the reader. According to the strata-theory of Ingarden, in the work of art itself objects are only given schematically, fragmentarily, in perspectives chosen by the author. It is up to the reader to make them complete in the form of a concretization. This study employs a contemporary variant of Ingarden's theory, the implied reader of Wolfgang Iser, which investigates this need for turning the sketch into a complete form in the concrete with the help of imagined experience and much else besides, as world-experiencing life. In Iser's view it is the *unformulated* aspects of the text that allow us to formulate a response to the aesthetic object, that we come to feel as the life of a fantastic world, its ideas, values, and specific intangible glamour. Thus it is not simply an array of linguistic structures or formalist devices to which we respond, though they are part of it to be sure. We respond to a world.

As a corollary to the formal imagination, there is a second reason for a phenomenological study. Since fantasy and science fiction are narrative arts, the tendency among theorists has been, understandably, to be primarily concerned with the various forms that plots may take in these genres. But as far as the reading process itself is concerned, narrative and the resources of form only satisfy one particular cluster of related desires. They silhouette the material of the fantasy world with a certain degree of clarity and thereby aid in the communication and perception of expressive content.

There is, however, another cluster of desires in reading, long recognized by phenomenological aestheticians and termed the material imagination. They seek satisfaction in the richness and sensuous exuberance of the imagined world. Of course I recognize that narrative itself does function through delays and counter-movements, intent on prolonging everything, but in general its function is to sweep us along towards a predestined end. But in reading fantasy and science fiction we often want to linger in those strange and exotic landscapes, even to luxuriate in them. Especially in utopian fiction, to which this study devotes one rather longish chapter, do we want to linger. Indeed the central aesthetic problem of the utopian novel has been how to make the reader feel what it is actually like to live in a utopia. This related cluster of desires seeking satisfaction in the material imagination of a fantastic world gives rise to an area of response known to phenomenologists as reverie. For reasons that will become more apparent later on in this introduction, only they have concerned themselves with analyzing in depth the significance of this area of our response in a non-reductive manner. The work of Gaston Bachelard, the French philosopher, is seminal in this respect, and I shall have a lot more to say about his writings presently.

A third reason for a phenomenological approach is one that for the moment can only be presented negatively: reverie is both core and method in the fantasy of Ray Bradbury, but it has not been studied. Bradbury has not fared well at the hands of those critics who disparage reverie as an aesthetic response. For instance, W. R. Irwin's rhetoric of fantasy, *The Game of the Impossible* (1976) argues that reverie is incoherent and non-cognitive because it is not "intellectual play."[5] The reader's role in fantasy according to this study consists in being persuaded by the implied author's rhetorical strategies to play with an "anti-fact." Because it contains no intellectual play, Irwin gives Bradbury's *Fahrenheit 451* as an example of what fantasy is *not,* namely, science fiction. But if we consult Darko Suvin's *Metamorphoses of Science Fiction* (1979), for an account of Bradbury's contribution to this genre we will be disconcerted. Not only is Bradbury perceived by Suvin to be unworthy of the term "science fiction," but because his texts belong to a monstrous and misshapen subgenre of true science fiction, "science-fantasy," they must also renounce any cognitive claims on the reader.[6] Either way, it would seem that reverie has no positive poetics in a field where everyone is his own Aristotle.

It is not my intention to belabor the obvious pitfalls of genre criticism, how it tends to mask hatred of a literary kind behind what should be a purely descriptive theoretical apparatus. It is interesting to note however how Suvin's generic rules become subtly prescriptive, defining realms of ideology. According to Suvin (who offers no readings from Bradbury's work to substantiate his claims) true science fiction is that fiction in which an estranging socio-historical *novum* (novelty or innovation; the term is Ernst Bloch's) is then validated for the reader by the exercise of scientific logic. Suvin's idea of the *novum,* although it is cast in a Marxist-structuralist framework, explicitly recognizes the role of new historical content in the reader's response. On the surface it therefore seems somewhat less reductive than the other views discussed above. But only a very small number of science-fiction stories actually follow this schema, if any. Even Arthur C. Clarke, an acknowledged master of hardcore science-fiction writing, does not always follow the dictates of scientific validation in his writing.[7] I will deal further with this view of the reader's role in science fiction in chapter 5, but here allow me to express my doubts that on the other hand fantasy literature produced in capitalist societies is as universally retrograde as Suvin supposes. At this point I can only repeat the open gesture of Georg Lukacs, arguably the greatest Marxist critic of the twentieth century, when he affirmed that "free play of the creative imagination and unrestrained fantasy are compatible with the Marxist conception of realism. Among the literary achievements Marx especially valued are the fantastic tales of Balzac and E.T. A. Hoffmann."[8] In this study I plan to show how reverie, far from being incoherent, abstract or vague, the last recourse of bourgeois idealism, is the very means by which we come to know the pulsating phenomena of historical and social life of Bradbury's fantastic worlds.

But if recent critics of both science fiction and fantasy have shunted Bradbury's texts from one camp to another without any clear perception of what is at stake in his work, there are nonetheless some encouraging signs of understanding. The most sensible assessment of Bradbury's place in science fiction seems to be that of Rabkin and Scholes in their *Science Fiction: History, Science, Vision* (1977). Not interested, as they say, in drumming anyone out of the science-fiction corps, they limit themselves to noting that Bradbury's special preserve is an extreme of elegiac sentiment and gentle fantasy touched with the eerie and uncanny:

> He has borrowed the externals of science fiction to disguise and make more convincing his magical preoccupations. Though much acclaimed, his books have worn less well than others, originally less noticed. The sentimentality, the too easy liberal moralizing, have been overtaken by events. And horror wears less well than thought. For a time it seemed as if Bradbury was making science fiction respectable to a larger circle of readers, but then it became less and less like science fiction.[9]

Scholes and Rabkin are obviously working on a variant of a psychoanalytical theory of literary response when they suggest that in Bradbury the external conventions of science fiction (robots, time travel, rocket ships, encounters with aliens, etc.) are only a disguise for a hidden world of fantasy, that by implication is still the source of his appeal. In my opinion, this observation is certainly true, though limited in that it leaves us at a loss to find a non-reductive method to study and display this world of magical preoccupations as having independent value.

Of course, given the survey character of their book, one would not expect an in-depth exploration of this world or any analysis of how it is communicated to the reader. However, Rabkin has recently produced a sensitive reading of *The Martian Chronicles* which attempts to relate the magical nature of Bradbury's Martian landscape to a style which he calls "crystalline description," borrowing insights from Max Lüthi and J. R. R. Tolkien about how the fairy tale works its enchantment on us.[10] Rabkin convincingly shows how Bradbury uses image-clusters of lyricism to drive the plot, set the mood, and comment on character. But again, if Bradbury's Mars is enchanted, we are not told how the reader takes over this world, making it his own, except that Rabkin allows that Bradbury is making a covert appeal to what Freud called the child's omnipotence of thought. But then so does every fantasy of this sort. We are left with no definite insight into what is specific about the reader's role in this world, or its relationship to history. Nevertheless, Rabkin's effort represents a step in the right direction because it identifies in Bradbury's style a concern and preoccupation with material images.

One of Rabkin's critical sources, Max Lüthi, calls this style of the fairy tale by its psychoanalytic name: sublimation. And indeed his analysis of the fairy tale is pretty much a psychoanalytic one. In *Once Upon a Time* (1970) Lüthi also demonstrates how the material imagination predominates in this literary form and gives us some indications about the role it plays in our response. According to Lüthi, in the fairy tale things which are in reality weighty and difficult become light and transparent, even volatile. The fairy tale sublimates reality. Lüthi correctly points out that this stylized world of perceptions and sensuous imaginings is therefore not a loss of reality, but rather a gain in the mastery of life, a freedom. The reader of the fairy tale imagines a world of gold, silver, and glass, those neatly fashioned material images which make feelings and valued relationships congeal into objects outwardly visible, making the world of the tale more easily assimilable to the reader. In this manner, the fairy tale "bestows on its hearer, *without him being aware of it* [my italics], something of its unaffected precision and brilliance."[11] Thus in Lüthi's view through material imagination, the world of the fairy tale is woven with the archetypal patterns of the cosmos (earth, air, fire, water), which are communicated to man in a manageable and beneficial form.

So if Bradbury's fantasy manifests a sublimative style, as Rabkin has argued, then this style should be linked to the reading process, in a manner Lüthi suggests. I have underlined in Lüthi's text an important aspect of image production in reading—normally it takes place effortlessly and rapidly, below the threshold of consciousness. This mental situation of images in reading is not, however, a reason to foreclose the study and analysis of how they are in fact constituted. They can be gotten at and brought to light by phenomenological methods which treat our interaction with literature as an act of consciousness. In a moment I am going to take up two phenomenological thinkers, Gaston Bachelard, who investigates the reader's sublimations, and Wolfgang Iser, who has been concerned with analyzing precisely how a network of images as acts of consciousness results from the nature of the text as a response-inviting structure, and show how such a method can be used in the study of fantasy literature. Both of these thinkers conceive of the image as an activity stimulating our response to a fictional world as does J. R. R. Tolkien, the other critical source of Rabkin's insight into Bradbury's style and its effect on the reader. I would like to discuss

Tolkien's ideas briefly before going on to Iser and Bachelard for the significance of what he says about the reader's role in creating a fantastic world.

In his essay "On Fairy-Stories" Tolkien tells us that fantasy begins with images of things not only "not actually present," but also not to be found in our primary world at all—that is the essence of their freedom as an unformulated reality. As Tolkien explains it, if a fairy tale speaks of bread or stone or tree, it appeals to the whole of these things in their independence, to their ideas, yet each reader will give to them a peculiar personal embodiment in his own imagination. Tolkien thus implies that this process (which he calls Recovery) is a double one. The reader is both himself, his personal associations, and the archetypal role he is called on to play in the fantasy text:

> Creative fantasy, because it is mainly trying to do something else (make something new), may open your hoard and let all the locked things fly away like cage-birds. The gems all turn into flowers or flames, and you will be warned that all you had (or knew) was dangerous and potent, not really effectively chained, free and wild; no more yours than they were you.
>
> The "fantastic" elements in verse and prose of other kinds, even when only decorative or occasional, help in this release. But not so thoroughly as a fairy story, a thing built on or about Fantasy, of which Fantasy is the core. Fantasy is made out of the Primary World, but a good craftsman loves his material, and has a knowledge and feeling for clay, stone and wood which only the art of making can give. By the forging of Gram cold iron was revealed; by the making of Pegasus horses were ennobled; in the Trees of the Sun and Moon root and stock, flower and fruit are manifested in glory.[12]

Tolkien is here contrasting his view of what creative fantasy does to and for the reader with that of the mere word-playfulness of Chestertonian fantasy which brings on only a momentary recovery of freshness of vision. If the reader is not really changed by the kind of sublimation specific to fantasy based on the material imagination, then we cannot speak of recovery in Tolkien's sense at all. It must involve what phenomenological thinkers call a "released spontaneity" in the reading subject, about which I will have more to say in the theoretical section of this study. It is not so much a binding or mastering of ours fears for us through the dragon-slaying of the story's action as it is a loosing or launching of the imagination. Again, we get the impression from this passage that a fantasy text has an unformulated double, especially when we discover to our surprise that we have mastered and are familiar with the world we thought was merely language, which turns out to be "no more yours than they (the word-images of the word-hoard) were you." Fantasy enables written words to transcend their literal meaning, to assume a multiple referentiality, and so to undergo the expansion necessary to transplant them as a new experience in the mind of the reader. In their archetypal aspects, therefore, the images of fantasy lie at the origins of enchantment. They should not then be treated as reified things, as Rabkin's formalist study of *The Martian Chronicles* tends to do, but rather as transformative acts of consciousness which condition our response to a fantastic world.

Both Tolkien and Lüthi imply that the reader's role in fantasy literature is hardly a simple one, certainly not as simple as that outlined for the generic reader in the studies we have mentioned. It must always be a complex, doubled affair, and there is no necessary reason why it need not be cognitive as well since it clearly has the potential to bring to consciousness things about ourselves that we did not know before. A recent article by F. C. Fredericks states, after examining four new theories of fantasy (Irwin, Rabkin, Manlove, and Todorov), that fantasy may use quite different but equally valid modes of cognition than science fiction and that we need to move theory nearer to actual fantasy texts by the production of closer readings of individual narratives.[13] What better way to bridge this gap than with a phenomenological theory that approaches literature through the reading process itself, seeking to spotlight and define the basic features of this complex interaction between reader and text?

What is needed, then, is a phenomenology of the fantastic, one which would suspend external classifications and deal with the experience of fantastic worlds as a process of self-discovery, historical understanding, and social criticism. By defining phenomenologically what the overall role of the reader in a fantasy text is (generic patterns will be a part of this, of course, but only a part), and then by investigating what happens to the reading subject as he is called upon to transform imaginatively that role, we will learn how our aesthetic response to a fantastic world is produced. Clearly, such a process cries out for analysis. And if there is a better way to approach the field of Bradbury's magical preoccupations and to demonstrate their appeal to the reader, then I am at a loss to know what it might be.

In the first chapters of this study I hope to compose with my own particular blend of two phenomenological thinkers just such a working method to deal with the complexity of the reader's role in Bradbury's fantasy. This working method will link the nature of reverie as an aesthetic response to a fantastic world with more historical notions of relationship between literature and society. The French philosopher and historian of science, Gaston Bachelard, provides the central category of "imaged reverie" used in this study as a model for a type of literary imagination operative in Bradbury's fantasy. A German philosopher of literature, Wolfgang Iser, enables us to describe in functional terms reverie as a pattern of communication between text and reader.

Using a distinction made by Robert Scholes in a review of Iser's *The Implied Reader* (1974), I have termed the first area of response sublimative, for Bachelard was concerned in his investigations to refine further the multifarious relations of self and world which fantasy presents.[14] His one consistent theme was that this type of literature teaches us how to dream onwards in metamorphoses of the material imagination, even to the limits of consciousness in our bodily sensuous contact with the world. A cognitive reader on the other hand is defined by his questioning of social norms, and this area of response is associated in Iser's work with the mainstream realistic novel and its transvaluation of social values.

These two areas of our response, the cognitive and the sublimative, can and should be brought together and studied in a cooperative way, especially if we are to understand utopian fiction which demands of us a total response, a dreaming forwards (or backwards) and social critique. This combination is also necessary because Bachelard was not himself disposed to discuss specific textual structures of the literary work of art. He used literature only to transcend it towards structures of imaginative consciousness, though of course there is a great deal of textual play in his own writings, which are a mass of citations and images. He was a very talented stage-manager of other writer's fantasies, and it is as reader of fantasy texts that Bachelard still has a lot to offer theorists interested in fantasy. Particularly valuable for students of fantasy are his analyses of the exotic flora and fauna of imaginary landscapes. In this regard, his lovely *L'Eau et les rêves* (1942), from which we are going to examine a passage in a moment, is most pertinent to the study of American fantasy for its analyses of Poe.

It has been noted that in the literature of romance, from which both science fiction and fantasy derive, setting typically receives much more emphasis than in realistic works where it is primarily a context for the portrayal of character: "The phenomenon of *landscape* as hero is particularly common in science fiction, where the truly active element of the story is frequently neither character nor plot but the world the writer creates . . ."[15] These landscapes were produced, Bachelard asserted, by authorial reverie faithfully pursued in one of the four archetypal elements: earth, air, fire, and water, or their combinations. Bachelard wrote a book each on air, fire, and water, and two books on the earth (see bibliography). Developing his own phenomenological method of reading, he showed that these landscapes possessed an oneiric logic of their own. In these books, Bachelard offers us unique insights into the managing of the aesthetic world of fantasy in terms of the subject in a landscape, as a means of drawing the reader into these worlds. It was Bachelard who, in these early studies, first brought the category of the material imagination into the field of modern aesthetics by showing how an author "materializes the fantastic."[16]

Since Bachelard's writings will not be as familiar to Anglo-American readers as Iser's, it is necessary at this point to provide a brief example of his working methods and a demonstration of what he means by the phrase "materialize the fantastic." Besides, reverie and reading are the main topics of this study and the best way to enter into the theoretical sections to come is to have some experience of it now. Readers of Poe's *The Adventures of A. Gordon Pym* will recall the episode in which the hero, Augustus Pym, first explores the savage island of Tsalal. The narrator, Pym himself, describes a fantastic water, purple and gum-like yet limpid, which flows in the streams of the island, saying in conclusion that "the phenomena of this water formed the first definite link in that vast chain of apparent miracles with which I was destined at length to be encircled."[17] So the water is linked by the narrator to narrative ground rules, but it is important to remember that we are told this at the end of a long passage of description. The first function of this water is, therefore, to draw us into the new world which is to be imagined. How does it do this, according to Bachelard?

Primarily by offering us a layer of significance which lies between two extremes most readers would reject: blood, which would probably displease or even repel us, and plain water, which is too ordinary to create a fantastic cosmos. In his analysis, Bachelard begins by observing that with *Pym* we seem to be in the midst of a very realistic story of shipwreck and adventure on the high seas:

> With Gordon Pym we are apparently at the opposite pole of inner life: adventures have to be geographical. But the narrator who starts with a descriptive tale feels the need to give an impression of strangeness. He must therefore invent; he must draw on his unconscious. Why could not water, that universal liquid, also take on a singular property? Discovered water will thus be an invented liquid. Invention, governed by the laws of the unconscious, suggests an organic liquid. It could be milk. But Poe's unconscious bears a particular, a fatal mark: valorization will be accomplished through blood. Here the consciousness intervenes: the word is not to be written on that page. Even if the word were to be pronounced, everything would rise up against it: consciousness would repress it, logically as an absurdity, experimentally as an impossibility, personally as an accursed memory. The extraordinary water which astonishes the traveler will then be an unnamed blood, an unnamable blood. So much for the analysis regarding the author.[18]

Bachelard next proceeds to discuss the reader, and how the page becomes readable for him. He points out that in the psychoanalytic theory of reader response, the page only becomes readable if the reader possesses the unconscious valorization of blood. If he does not, the page loses all significance; indeed, it is incomprehensible, a facile and arbitrary invention. There is, however, an independent layer of material imagination and reverie which elicits satisfactorily our desire to explore this new world. It is only later that Bachelard will draw on phenomenological methods to delimit this area of response, but here he clearly intends us to understand that reverie cannot be reduced to the unconscious Freudian fantasy, and he is quick to point out the limitations of Marie Bonaparte's analysis of Poe:

> However, classical psychoanalysis, whose lessons I followed in this particular interpretation, does not seem to account for all the imagery. It neglects the study of the intermediary zone between blood and water, between the unnamable and the named. It is precisely in this intermediary zone, where expression requires *many words,* that Poe's passage bears the mark of genuinely experienced liquids. It is not the unconscious that would suggest the experiment of slipping a knife between the veins of this extraordinary water. That requires a positive familiarity with *fibrillary* water, with a liquid which, although formless, has an internal structure and, as such, is the source of endless fascination to the material imagination [*amuse sans fin l'imagination matérielle*]. I believe that it is possible therefore to assert that during his childhood Poe was interested in jellies and gums. . . . It is possible that he dreamed of blood while kneading the gum, but it is because he did this—as many others have done— that he did not hesitate to put into a *realistic* narrative rivers that flow slowly, that in flowing

maintain veins like thickened water. . . . Poe transposed limited experiences to a cosmic level. . . The heavy water *[l'eau lourde]* of Poe's metapoetics obviously has a *component* drawn from a very childish physics.[19]

I have omitted sections from this exemplary analysis which describe the remarkable joy and sense of well-being that Bachelard ascribes to the stirring and pulling of such a substance, a pleasure associated with childhood and the unrepressed body, as all Bachelardian reverie is. I will have more to say about the body as the site of reverie in later chapters. What I want to emphasize now about this passage is that it tells us that reverie is best studied phenomenologically. Bachelard considers the fantastic phenomena of Poe's *Pym* as descriptions of an actual life-world. Taking the perceptual and tactile imagined experience of Poe's "gum-like water" to say that I experience with joy a certain pleasure in kneading it would be the same thing, for the phenomenologist, as saying that the water "offers me a meaning" of a fantastic world. There is no need to reduce this phenomena to an underlying fantasy. That which shows itself to me is measured in terms of that which it is possible for me to say about it. A phenomena is thus identified with the sayable, hence the definition of phenomenology as the description of lived experience, and the need for many words that tell of an experience which in itself is mute. Reverie is best treated as a realm of imaginative experience that is transposed to the cosmic level, which offers us a world.

Bachelard in his early works sometimes refers to this layer of significance as the oneiric level of the text and I have followed his usage in this study in order to distinguish it from narrative and other textual perspectives. Indeed, it is the major contention of this study that Bradbury's fantasy texts eventually foreground the oneiric level, and ask the reader to perform his own reverie by linking together images produced by the structured blanks and negations of the text, its indeterminacies. Our reverie prolongs and metamorphoses these images, finally linking them together in a coherent aesthetic response to an imaginary world. Although Bachelard says that he does not know how to read a narrative objectively, in examining the writings of Poe he did offer some suggestions towards a "double reading" of the fantastic, one that would simultaneously follow the thread of the narrative and seek to discover how these events are to imagined at the oneiric level.

Bachelard implies that this oneiric level offers us a transcendental vantage point from which to understand a fantastic world (and a *fantastique transcendantale,* proposed, but never completed, would have defined the possibility of emergence of any fantastic world as the sublimation of an archetype). It is from this standpoint that Bachelard adopted a hermeneutic attitude towards images, asking himself under what oneiric impetus of the imagination the events of the story are to be imagined. Agreeable as it would be to discuss his speculations on Poe's fantasy for themselves, we cannot go into detail about them here, or discuss how Bachelard unfolds the oneiric logic of invention *(la logique onirique de l'in-*

vention) in Poe's *Pym,* especially as it pertains to the archetype of the labyrinth where Poe seems to totalize his reveries, both conscious and unconscious. Suffice it to say that according to Bachelard it is through reverie that Poe was able to transpose his personal obsessions to the cosmic level where "dreamer and universe together labor on the same work."[20] In Bachelard's phenomenological analysis of Poe's reveries, Poe remains a prodigious dreamer who was master of all his doublings.

Bachelard wanted an oneiric criticism for fantasy texts, one that he hoped would give back to them their imaginary stature, because he felt that this had been robbed from them by a host of reductive approaches from the narrowly philological to the psychoanalytically orthodox. In oneiric criticism, one performs a dreaming on the text *(rêve sur l'oeuvre).* One projects images initiated by the text back into the text again with the help of the specific ambience created by reverie. One prolongs and intensifies the act of reading itself. As a hermeneutical interaction and reading method, Bachelard's reading while dreaming *(lire en rêvant)* interprets dreams by the dreams we have in reading, which it then amplifies by bringing other oneiric documents and citations into play. It is this reading method that I hope to modify and use in this study.

No doubt this method, used as it stands, is much too subjective to suit accepted views of what criticism is supposed to do. Yet it is of the greatest value for the study of our response to fantastic literature. Bachelard has often been assimilated to a kind of thematology (as in the pages devoted to him in Todorov's *The Fantastic*) or to archetypal criticism (as in Northrop Frye's introduction to *The Psychoanalysis of Fire*), which indicates that his work is of continuing importance. And in the light of recent reader-response criticism it is evident that his real emphasis was on the reader throughout all his work, even if he did not often treat whole works, as he does in the case of Poe's *Pym.* I myself find that reverie needs to be investigated in a more scrupulously text-centered way if we are going to define how it communicates. But we cannot blame Bachelard for not having a theory of the text when other critics of his day hardly even mentioned the reader. In retrospect, his work seems ahead of its time.

Complementary to Bachelard's interest in the phenomenology of imaginative consciousness if Wolfgang Iser's investigation of the ways in which novels set up certain limits within which we respond. For Iser, as for Bachelard, the imagination plays a central role in the reader's discovery of the "living event" which is the text's world. But unlike Bachelard, Iser points out that if the text did not stimulate our desire to picture under unfamiliar conditions (whereas Bachelard is quite certain of the familiarity of the material imagination), we would never set off to discover a new reality, one which is also implicitly a criticism of deficiencies inherent in the norms and conventions of the society which form the background of the novel. In Iser's view, a work of narrative fiction impinges on both historical conditions and social realities—indeed, it is largely a response to, and a reading of, those conditions. Although he has been concerned with realistic fiction, Iser's main theme in *The Implied Reader* (1974), the reader's self-discovery, is admirably suited to the study of fantasy literature as well. For it is only by leaving behind the familiar world of our everyday experience that the reader can truly participate in the adventure the text offers him. The archetype of reading is the quest, as he says in his chapter on Joyce's *Ulysses.*[21]

I hope to be able to adapt Bachelard's theory of the literary imagination to Iser's theory of the reading process, without losing Bachelard's critical objectives and without demolishing Iser's framework, in order to evaluate the specific nature of the fantasy texts in question: poetic reverie unfolding in narrative. This blend of Iser and Bachelard should not be unduly distorting, if we do not force either thinker to give up what is essential to him: for Iser, the investigation of textual structures and structured acts of consciousness that define the reader's cognitive role in a text, and for Bachelard the oneiric level of our response to fantasy literature, which reveals our desire for a realm of fantastic beauty. Thus we should be able to study the literary image as an act of consciousness which is also an emotive-cognitive synthesis.

I have borrowed certain notions from Bachelard's proposed *fantastique transcendantale.* As the reader will find out in subsequent chapters, I intend them to be taken purely as heuristic notions. They are the archetypes of earth, air, fire, and water which are the implied foundations of Bachelard's reverie complexes. I have also borrowed categories from his phenomenological descriptions of structures of imaginative consciousness that are discussed in his later works, *The Poetics of Reverie* (1960) and *The Poetics of Space* (1958). These are object reverie *(rêverie d'objet)*, reverie towards childhood *(rêverie vers l'enfance)*, and cosmic reverie *(rêverie cosmique).* All of these Bachelardian notions are then inserted into the general framework of the reading process according to Iser.

This study is then intended to be Bachelardian, for all these structures of consciousness can be found in Bradbury's fantasy together with the affects Bachelard records: the feeling of well-being and ontological security *(bien-être)*, the ecstasy and gentle boredom of the child, the surging of memories from childhood, the ennoblement of matter in cosmic reverie, and the doublings of imaginative consciousness in flights of elated sublimation. They are, in brief, the field of Bradbury's magical preoccupations. Rather than study these structures absolutely, and hence to reify them, I have elected to give a brief outline of the reverie in question immediately before or during the analysis of each text. In this manner we can have it fresh in mind during the reading process and determine how Bradbury departs from or makes use of it for the purpose of oblique social criticism (i.e., for cognitive reasons).

In the presentation of oneiric readings of Bradbury's fantasy stories I rely on Bachelard to show what reverie is, and on Iser's heuristic model of the implied reader to demonstrate how it functions in a narrative context and is communicated. The selections from Bradbury are intended to be representative of the range and generative function of reverie in his work, though I am by no means trying to set up a Bradbury canon. One chapter each is devoted to the contribution that reverie makes to the marvelous, the Gothic, the science-fiction, and the utopian strains in his work. The chapters are arranged in sequence according to the degree of complexity of the reader's role, from simple object reverie in "The Sea Shell" to the utopian novel, *Fahrenheit 451.*

As in all reader-response criticism, the intention is to remain faithful to the actual experience of reading where the meaning of the text is produced. So what in standard critical analyses are considered features of the work itself are here described as an evolving temporal process of anticipation, frustration, retrospection, and reconstruction. Genres are no longer taxonomic classes but groups of norms and expectations which help the reader assign functions to various elements in the work. Plot is less a structure of objective logic that exists outside the text than it is a construction of the reader based on the demands of signification. Character in this study is treated as an organizing complex in the reader's mind which attempts to control the flow of meaning. Finally, phenomenological theorists such as Iser affirm that the author's intentional acts constrain the reader by providing a repertoire of patterns serving and overall strategy through which the text's world is to be presented. Yet since the text contains "gaps" or indeterminate areas, it offers incentives as well as constraints.

1

Wolfgang Iser and the Cognitive Reader

Wolfgang Iser has introduced in his *The Act of Reading* (1978) an idealized model of text-processing constructed along broadly phenomenological lines. He refers to it as the implied reader, "a transcendental model which makes it possible for the structured effects of literary texts to be described."[1] This model furthermore denotes the role of the reader as defined by two complementary aspects, in terms of textual structure and in terms of the structured acts of consciousness we deploy in grasping the meaning of a text. This bipartite model may account for a certain repetitiousness in Iser's critical readings in *The Implied Reader*—a tendency I have tried, not altogether successfully, to avoid. In any case the important thing is that meaning is not viewed as something that exists independently in the text, but as something which must be ideated by the mind of the reader, an event which he later calls the experience of the imaginary.

The central function of the novel, according to Iser, lies in its potential to make the reader through this experience aware of his familiar norms and codes, and thereby to effect a certain degree of liberation from the limitations of his accustomed views and beliefs. Iser demonstrates that the novel requires its readers to reconstruct their own social values through an accommodation to the negation of social norms provided by the novel as an agent of cognition. Iser's reader is, therefore and as Robert Scholes indicates, having an experience mainly cognitive rather than sublimative. The implied reader must value texts for their newness—either for their significant differences from their predecessors or, more subtly, their ability to generate perpetually new readings in a tradition through their own cognitive richness.

Iser argues that in order for the literary text to have these potential effects, it must have certain properties. It has to invoke and at the same time problematize, question, and even negate the reader's expectations (including, or course, generic expectations). It must make him aware of their limitations, and also make him imagine something new as a solution to these discovered deficiencies. It is this very intricate, dynamic process between text and reader that Iser attempts to explain on every page of *The Act of Reading,* but I have chosen to emphasize for this study what is most important in his model for fantasy literature, namely, the process of image production and formation that accompanies the appearance of the aesthetic object, a fantastic world. By focusing on the "something new" that fantasy asks us to ideate, we can thereby show that fantasy literature can be cognitive as well as sublimative.

Since we are seeking to insert certain structures of Bachelardian reverie and fantasy into the general framework of Iser's theory, it is perhaps best to start with an overview of image production in the phenomenological view. For Bachelard the literary image was always essentially a novelty which brought about, if we remained sensitive to its nuances, an increment of consciousness. As a phenomenological thinker, Iser maintains the difference between ideation and perception of an object as important for the study of the reading process because in a novel there is no given object to be perceived; instead the object must be built up from the knowledge invoked by a sequence of textual schemata. It is this operation—common, according to Iser, to every act of reading—that lifts the reader out of the situation he was in prior to reading. The experience of the imaginary removes him from everyday life, takes him away from actuality. The image in this process, though an act of consciousness, is normally a passive synthesis (one in which a quality of ego is not actively present as an orienting pole) occurring below the threshold of consciousness when we read and as a result of our attempt to build up a consistent pattern or picture of some object, person, event, etc., in the portrayed world. As we mentioned in our introduction, both Max Lüthi and J. R. R. Tolkien recognize this process as being essential to the effect of fantasy, though of course they do not use the technical terms of phenomenology to describe it. This process of consistency-building actually gives shape to the reader's own imaginary identity as he travels inside the frame of the portrayed world and executes the instructions given to him. Indeed, in Iser's view the meaning effects of a work of literature can *only* be experienced and grasped as this intermediary situation in which images are produced and refined comes into play. Images are the meeting place between text and reader. The reader produces the imaginary meaning that the text potentially structures, and only then does he try to incorporate this imaginary meaning into his own familiar framework, determining the significance of this new experience for himself in a later phase of comprehension. If the reader is to respond to the text at all, whether he accepts the role he is given to play or rejects it, it is clear that the reader cannot detach himself from such an interaction. Imagination in reading represents the basic condition of communication between text and reader.

Accordingly, the cognitive image produced by the reader is conditioned by the play of familiar and unfamiliar. Since this play—emphasized and made visible—is crucial to the effect of fantasy, I will now bring out the most important aspects of the phenomenological view of literature's defamiliarizing or deautomatizing properties. This effect in Iser's account is produced in part by rhetorical structures, such as those outlined in Wayne Booth's *The Rhetoric of Fiction,* in particular, the accord or discord between an implied author and the role he asks the reader to play.[2] In Wayne Booth's view, and more recently W. R. Irwin in *The Game of the Impossible,* the reader-in-the-text is always a double figure. He is both a credulous or "pretending" person who must at least entertain the values of the implied author if he is to interact successfully with the text, and a doubter. The first figure could be said to accept all the moves required, including fantastic steps, such as Kafka's turning Gregor Samsa into a beetle in "The Metamorphosis," and incredible beliefs, always present in the fairy tale or romance, such as "people live happily ever after." For Booth the second figure is a more sophisticated ambassador from the real world, one who is able to permit or even encourage the credulous activity of his twin and who knows all the while that some parts of what is embraced during the reading of fantasy do not accord with his beliefs back in the real world.

The difficulty with this rhetorical view of fantasy literature is, however, that the reader can never be estranged in any cognitive way during reading because, according to this model, he already knows all the while and from the beginning what his role is. Indeed, this is the very conclusion Irwin comes to. *The Game of the Impossible* asserts that the logic of fantasy denies any privilege to ambiguity, that the reader must be at home in the narrative world at all times by knowing what "anti-fact" is being asserted and persuasively developed, and that fantasy therefore never comes to a surprise ending. Furthermore, "nothing of any conceptual validity is destroyed or overturned by it."[3]

Now, Iser is willing to accept the tension produced by such an interaction between the reader's role and a real reader whose personality, norms, and expectations he does not want to exclude. To do so would be to deny the text's impingement on real historical conditions. Indeed for Iser it is this very tension or dissonance which leads to the reader's self-discovery. But Iser asserts that in his model the reader has to first produce the image of the implied author if he is to react to it. A phenomenological account of the implied reader, we can also add, should therefore have logical priority over any account of a generic reader posited for all fantasy texts, because it remains closer to the origins of the fantastic in studying the process of building up a world.

In Iser's view rhetoric, if it is to be successful, requires a clearly formulated purpose (in Irwin's terminology, an "anti-fact"). But it is Iser's main point about reading that the text takes an already formulated social reality and presents it in an essentially estranged way so that the reader is forced to ideate something new, to search for hidden causes behind this deformation, in order to comprehend it. Furthermore, each new concretization also participates obliquely in the historical situation to which the text is in part a reaction. Through its familiar repertoire (a structured part of the text we will define in a moment), the text has already entered into the reader's horizon of expectations. Or, conversely, the reader already stands within the text's circle of interpretation. It comes to him as something to be understood and to be brought into a dialogue, a game of questions and answers.

Yet this play does not therefore leave the reader's intellectual assumptions unquestioned, as Irwin believes. Irwin fails to acknowledge an important aspect of Wayne Booth's implied author (indeed the concept is never once mentioned in this book although the influence of neo-Aristotelian criticism in general is evident), one that perhaps would have been fatal for his view of the reader's role in fantasy. For Booth argues that some beliefs are for the implied author fixed, and some are not. The image of the implied author as a core of norms guarantees that some values or "anti-facts" not only can be applied to the real world but should be. True, some are meant to be only provisional for the duration of reading, but since what is required of the reader in Irwin's rhetoric of fantasy is belief in an impossibility anyway, this belief is to be shucked off after reading without any ethical effect. Irwin fails to explain why a text such as Kafka's "The Metamorphosis," which he singles out for analysis, should be of concern to us. Surely fantasy literature is more than just a game. Implicit in Iser's notion of self-discovery is the view that we learn about forgotten dimensions of our being, which can lead to an examination of ethical values as well.

In any case rhetoric, in the sense of Wayne Booth or W. R. Irwin, may provide a guide which influences the reader to produce the meaning of the text, but for Iser the reader's participation goes far beyond the scope of this influence because the formulated text (composed of repertoire and strategies) shades off, through allusion and suggestion, into a text that is open to possibilities of imaginative transformation, though nonetheless intended.

Iser levels essentially the same criticism at psychoanalytic theories of reader response which assert that literature offers us what is essentially comfort, escape, and the relief of emotional tensions produced by the activation of unconscious and asocial fantasies in reading. In the view of emotive theorists such as Norman Holland or Simon O. Lesser, a work of art does indeed become meaningful in proportion to the intensity with which it engages conflicting agencies of the psyche (the Freudian ego, id, and superego) in a transformation of an unconscious core of fantasy towards meaning. The push towards a familiar intellectual theme that a reader may feel in reading is shown by these theorists to be analogous to sublimation. Literary form is defense; literary images on the other hand awaken unconscious fantasies.

Yet Iser does not object to the concept of a sublimative reader. What he objects to is the reified use of psychoanalytic terminology, I think justly, for images in Holland's dictionary of fantasy are simply things which serve to awaken the reader's latent interest in a particular fantasy associated with a stage of sexual organization: oral, anal, phallic, etc. Thus images of dirt or of being dirtied are the clue to unconscious anal fantasies, their aims and satisfactions.[4] Now, there is no doubt that fantasy literature, including reverie, operates with unconscious fantasies, but as I try to show in the next chapter, it transforms them in a manner that is something less than a disguise. Iser's criticism of psychoanalytic theories of the reading process is well taken: despite all the discussion of the uncanny with its play of familiar and unfamiliar, whether based on wish fulfillment or the mastery of anxiety through the formal properties of the work of art, the psychoanalytic theory offers the reader nothing new. The reader beholds a Platonic mirror image of himself (Iser might have invoked narcissism, but the point is clear enough). For Holland in particular a work of art reflects the various dispositions of its readers, their identity theme.[5]

For Iser, the entire process of textual comprehension is set in motion by the need to familiarize the unfamiliar, to search for imagistic unformulated equivalences to a new presentation. Hence the presence, in almost every period of literary history, of some technique of defamiliarization, a strategy which negates familiar and habitual perceptions in order to make us more aware of ourselves and our surroundings.[6] Literature would be barren, Iser asserts, if it led only to recognition of the familiar. The reader needs the unknown and unformulated factors in the text to set off on his quest, and it is only when the reader is forced to produce the meaning of the text under unfamiliar conditions (rather than his own conditions, that is, by analogizing his life to that of the portrayed world) that he can discover hitherto unknown facets of his personality.

This concludes our discussion of one pole of Iser's implied reader, that of structured acts of consciousness. Now we will go over the same ground in terms of textual structure. What, then, are the main components of the text which stimulate the reader to formulate the experience of the imaginary which Iser describes? For Iser, this dynamic process of recreation is steered by two main structural components: first, a repertoire of familiar literary patterns and themes, together with allusions to familiar social norms and historical thought systems (thus the text prior to the reading process is already a "reading" of its social environment); second, techniques or strategies to set the familiar against the unfamiliar. These two aspects of the reality of fiction define the novel as a communicatory structure for Iser. We will discuss the repertoire first.

There are two components to the repertoire, which reshapes familiar schemata to form a background for the process of communication and provides a general framework within which the message or meaning of the text can be organized. First of all, the text is a selection from the social norms of everyday life and the dominant ideological systems of thought of the day. This is the text's relation to reality; it does not copy or describe so much as present a reaction to the dominant thought system. Fiction and reality are thus not mutually exclusive opposites; rather, literature is the complement of reality, it tells us about reality (in the form of a penumbra of other suppressed thought systems) and it is correlated with it. Iser theorizes that because it is a *selection* of norms, the repertoire does not reproduce exactly the prevalent thought system. Instead, it excludes the frame of reference within which these norms are stabilized. In Iser's language, it "depragmatizes" them. This reaction is triggered by the fact of any system's limited ability to cope with the multifariousness of reality. The text tends to take as its dominant "meaning" those possibilities that have been neutralized or negated by the dominant thought system or the norms of everyday life. Thus it draws attention to deficiencies, and its basic reference is to "the penumbra of excluded possibilities" along the borderlines of existing systems. The reader is compelled to ask what principle governs the selection of these norms, cultural conventions, or moral principles, and the nature of this questioning is one factor in determining the implied reader's portrait.

The second part of the repertoire which aids in this determination is the selection of literary allusions to traditions of past literature. They are depragmatized in the same way as the norms, for again they are functional, not merely imitative, even if they are drawn from a different system composed of past literary reactions to historical problems instead of historical thought systems themselves. If the selection of norms points out deficiencies then the function of literary allusions is to aid in producing an answer to the problems set by the deficiencies. The allusions "quote" earlier answers to the problem; they are a means for generalizing the repertoire's relation to the social totality and the reasons for selections because they reshape familiar schemata of literary genres and impose an unfamiliar dimension of literary history on the rhythm of image production.

Consequently, the two selections from outside or extra-textual reality are set against each other: the reality of social norms and values which present a problem or deficiency is set against literary allusions, schemas and archetypes which suggest, but do not formulate, an answer. The reader therefore searches for equivalences between the two elements, which do not always bear the same degree of familiarity, projecting images one into the other in a process that Iser calls "coherent deformation," borrowing from Merleau-Ponty's phenomenological theory of meaning.[7] In summary, we may say that the repertoire is the way in which the text impinges on historical and social reality. It provides us with a means to assess a crucial area of our response that is lacking in the theories of fantasy mentioned in our introduction, the dimension of history. The overall function of the repertoire is to provide familiar grounds for the reassessment of reality; it sets up a parallel frame or organizational structure within which meaningful patterns are to form, and grounds the reader in the intersubjective goal of the text: "the imaginary correction of deficient realities."[8]

If the repertoire is a selection from familiar "outside" reality, then there must also be a means of combination of literary allusions and norms within the text and a way of mediating them to the reader so that he can produce the equivalences they suggest. The strategies organize the actualization of the system of equivalences, the internal perspectives and network of references whose ultimate function is to defamiliarize the familiar. The basic structure of the strategies arises out of the selective composition of the repertoire itself, which inevitably creates a background-foreground relationship of tension with the chosen element in the foreground evoking its original background setting. The chosen element (in parody a literary allusion, for instance) evokes its original setting, but it is to take on a new and as yet unknown function. Here the play of familiarity and unfamiliarity is the condition for all further forms of comprehension in the narrative, for the yet unknown meaning would be incomprehensible were it not for the familiarity of the background it is set against.

The second main strategy for setting the familiar against the unfamiliar is properly a syntagmatic one, the structure of theme and horizon. The pattern of the repertoire emerges through a kaleidoscopic combination of four different perspectives: that of the characters, that of the narrator, that of the plot and that marked out for the fictitious reader (not to be confused with the implied reader; this is a textual strategy, an embodiment of particular, contemporary reading attitudes and dispositions, frequently addressed directly by the text). All these perspectives are interwoven in the text and offer a constantly shifting constellation of views during the time-flow of reading. It is therefore impossible for the reader to grasp the world of the text entirely from one homogeneous perspective. The view that the reader is involved with at any particular moment is the theme, conditioned by the familiar horizon of other perspective segments in which he had been situated previously. This means that the image is always open also to a horizon of possibilities that includes the memory of past images and the promise of future transformations.

In this manner, and not from simple "willing suspension of disbelief" (often invoked in formalist studies such as Rabkin's), do we come to take over the author's unfamiliar view of the world on terms laid down by the author. The structure of theme and horizon involves us actively in the process of searching for equivalences among the perspectives and shifting viewpoints. In a process of anticipation and retrospection which builds a network of intentionalities, viewpoints modify one another, influencing past and future syntheses. Each narrative segment is thus a "two-way glass," is both itself and a reflector and illuminator of the others. Gradually, according to Iser (and this may be a residue in his theory of classical norms of interpretation) they begin to offer the reader a "transcendental vantage point" from which he can see through all the positions and doublings that have been formulated.[9] The resultant accumulation of imagistic equivalences and the emergence of the transcendental vantage point mark the appearance of the aesthetic object, which in turn constitutes our response to the world of the text. Some fantasy texts may deliberately frustrate this transcendental vantage pont (Kafka, for example), but in fantasy texts based on reverie we expect the oneiric level of the text to provide indications as to how the events of the story are to be imagined.

Thus the efficacy of the literary text is brought about by the apparent evocation and subsequent negation of the familiar. Elements of the repertoire are continually backgrounded or foregrounded, overmagnified, trivialized, or negated by the strategies. This defamiliarization of what the reader expected or thought he recognized leads him to intensify his expectations as well as distrust them at the same time, after the defeat of expectations. Rabkin's reversal of ground rules is one strategy used by the fantastic; Todorov's doubt or hesitation is another. In this manner, there arises a process of illusion-forming and illusion-breaking which makes reading an essentially recreative and imaginative process. We familiarize the unfamiliar through illusion-building. The process is, as Iser presents it in an earlier account of the implied reader. "virtually hermeneutic."[10] The text provokes certain expectations which we in turn project into the text in order to reduce the polysemantic possibilities of the text to a single configurative meaning. In short, we need to make the experience offered to us by the text accessible to us, and we make use of illusion-building to make it readable.

In some modern texts, such as Joyce's *Ulysses,* this desire to picture arises continually. In his analysis, Iser demonstrates for us the reader's continual search for equivalences between the Homeric allusions and the events of Bloom's life.[11] In order to close up situations and comprehend the unfamiliar, we seek for consistency, for a "gestalt" between these two systems. Iser asserts that this is a living process, one in which we are forced to make selective decisions and become involved in the textual pattern we ourselves have produced. Reading thus reflects the structure of experience to the extent that we must open ourselves up to the workings of the text, leave behind our expectations, and suspend the ideas and attitudes that have shaped our personality before we can experience the unfamiliar world of the text. Joyce's *Ulysses* has the effect of making us more aware of how we experience the multifarious pattern of everyday life around us. In short, something unformulated happens to us during the reading process which leads to self-discovery. The way in which we habitually perceive things is reorganized by aesthetic effects, revealing the openness of the world.

With regard to the epistemological position of the subject in reading, we have already observed that the reading process suspends the subject-object division that otherwise is an assumed prerequisite for all knowledge and observation of a cognitive kind. This puts reading in an apparently unique position as regards the possible absorption of new experiences. Our way into the world of the text, and our relations with it, are similar to the process of indentification described by psychoanalysis. We establish affinities between ourselves and someone outside ourselves, usually the hero of the story. In this way, we build familiar ground on which to experience the unfamiliar. Now, Iser does not deny that identification is a form of participation as we read. However, he points out that an author's aim is usually to convey experience and, above all, an attitude towards that experience, so identification is not an end in itself, but a strategem by means of which the author stimulates attitudes in the reader.

Above all, Iser wants to preserve the tension between the real and the implied reader. He remarks in his view of this split: "As we read, there occurs an artificial division of our personality, because we take as a theme for ourselves something we are not."[12] For Iser, what we are will never disappear completely from the reading of a text. We can only make someone else's thoughts into an absorbing theme for ourselves provided our own virtual background can adapt to it: indeed, as we have tried to show in this brief and very selective outline of Iser's ideas, it is the relationship between the alien theme of a text and the virtual background of ourselves which makes it possible for the unfamiliar to be understood. There may very well be wish-fulfillment in novels, plays and poems, but rather than suppose that we gratify our desire by some mechanism of vicarious experience, Iser attempts to demonstrate how a text enables us to *formulate* our desires by bringing into play our faculty of imagination. Imagination and the text remain open. We cannot totalize the meaning of a text, but rather we discover for ourselves the role of active imagination in our lives—or at least this is what I assert for fantasy texts based on reverie. In this regard Iser also remarks: "Herein lies the dialectical structure of reading. The need to decipher gives us a chance to formulate our own deciphering capacity, i. e., we bring to the fore an element of our being of which we are not directly conscious."[13]

In Iser's view, the author can only hope to convey his intention by activating the reader's imagination and involving him in the world of the text. His intention must to a large degree remain unformulated, as an indeterminacy, for "indeterminacy is the force which drives us to work out a configurative meaning while at the same time giving us the necessary degree of freedom to do so."[14] It is something of a paradox, but Iser affirms that meaning coincides with the emergence of the reverse side of the represented world.

Iser assumes, however, that all imagistic syntheses take place below the threshold of consciousness unless they are raised above this threshold for the sake of analysis. As we shall see in the next chapter, this is exactly what reverie does in order to give us access to a fantastic world.

2

Gaston Bachelard and
the Sublimative Reader

At the end of the last chapter we approached again the subject of the so-called passive syntheses in reading, the imagistic means by which we take over the unfamiliar world of the fantasy text, and which take place along the time axis of reading. Iser is quick to point out, however, that the expression "passive synthesis" would be a contradiction in terms if it merely denoted processes of acceptance and composition that took place *automatically* below the threshold of consciousness.[1] Iser wishes to avoid any connotation of a mechanical quality belonging to those images which actually give rise to the "released spontaneity" of the self in reading. But how does it happen that the experience of images or the imaginary mobilizes the spontaneity of the subject?

Mainly, as we have seen, it is a result of the split that develops between the subject and himself during reading. The dichotomy which Iser posits for any reading experience, that between role and habitual orientation, results in a "contrapuntally structured personality" in reading.[2] This double role, which we will discuss for fantasy texts based on reverie a bit further on in this chapter, not only enables the subject to make himself present to the text, it also brings about an actual split in him, a kind of self-alienation, which indicates the extent to which the subject has been affected by the text. Affection stimulates the desire of the subject to regain the coherence he has lost through this doubling process; new experience has to be incorporated, hence the spontaneity of the subject is mobilized. But the foundation for this experience in which "something happens" to the reader is still the process of passive synthesis in which text and reader are linked together.

Now, for Bachelard also the experience of the imaginary gives rise to a spontaneity in the reading subject which can only be expressed as the desire and aspiration for new images. He called this desire to know and transform a fantastic world the material imagination:

> . . . this amazing need for *penetration* which, going beyond the attractions of the imagination of forms, thinks matter, dreams in it, lives in it, or, in other words, materializes the imaginary. I thought it justifiable to speak of a law of the four material imaginations which

necessarily attributes to a creative imagination one of the four elements: fire, earth, air, or water. Certainly, several elements can combine to form a particular image; there are *composite* images; but images have a life characterized by a purer line of filiation. Whenever images appear in series, they point to a primal matter, a fundamental element. The physiology of imagination, even more than its anatomy, is subject to the law of the four elements.[3]

For Bachelard, the sequence of images produced from a fantasy text open to reveal an underlying archetypal element that sustains the play of surface imagery. They stimulate our desire to penetrate further into this world. Not that the formal imagination is ignored by Bachelard's aesthetics: adornment and disguise are necessary for "the initial seduction of the reader," but it is the material imagination that provides the world with intimacy and depth, allowing the author's values to take on imaginative force.[4] What is more, this experience of intimacy at the heart of matter was for Bachelard always linked to the body, our childhood bodies, where the image is an act of the hand, a magical gesture working with valorized substances. Man in reverie is "man made dynamic by his work."[5] In Bachelardian reverie therefore there is none of that dreamy passiveness usually associated with the word reverie. Reverie is the exploration of a world, as in our example from Poe in the introduction.

We can now relate Bachelard's poetics of reading to Iser's framework if we elaborate on the experience of the imaginary, which is central to both thinkers. In summarizing Iser's argument, I said that we place our synthesizing faculties at the disposal of an unfamiliar reality, produce the meaning of that reality, and in so doing enter into a situation which we could not have created out of ourselves. We experience something new, which in the case of fantasy is the experience of the archetypally rich and strange, as Tolkien in his discussion of recovery so ably describes it. Iser himself has written of this experience in terms more cognitive than affective, but only because for him affection is a later stage of textual comprehension. The experience of this new meaning is not really semantic at all until it is incorporated into the reader's own familiar framework of understanding. It is an experience, the imaginary, which the subject has undergone, and in a recent article Iser replaces the somewhat awkward notion of a non-semantic meaning with that of the experience of the imaginary.[6] And so we should understand the term "meaning" in this passage from *The Act of Reading* where the relationship between the reader's desire and passive syntheses is explained:

> Thus the meaning of the literary text can only be fulfilled in the reading subject and does not exist independently of him; just as important, though, is that the reader himself, in constituting the meaning, is also constituted. And herein lies the full significance of the so-called passive synthesis.
>
> This experience is what underlies the reader's desire to comprehend the significance of the meaning. The ceaseless and inevitable quest for the significance shows that in assembling the meaning we ourselves become aware that something has happened to us, and so we try to find out its significance.[7]

The images constituted in reading are passive in the sense that something happens to the reader, but in Iser's model there is held out the promise that this experience will be converted into knowledge. Bachelard's investigations into the image-sequences of fantasy texts are clearly attempts to discover those chains of passive syntheses leading to the reader's experience of something new, the wonder and surprise of the oneiric image, to track them down with an awakened sensitivity. But Bachelard was mainly concerned with the "cosmology" of reverie, how it offers us a world if pursued faithfully. For Bachelard the reader's desire to comprehend the significance of the imaginary led to dialectical sublimation and the rediscovery of archetypal realities, once reverie had awakened them.

Bachelard coined the term "imagined image" to indicate that in dialectical sublimation the reader's released spontaneity is given a certain archetypal shape in reading.[8] Imagined images are sublimations of archetypes rather than reproductions of reality. The experience of the imaginary in reverie is therefore not derived from perception but from an existential encounter with primal realities. In addition, the experience of this archetypal reality has two phases of comprehension analogous to Iser's: that of the physical, which Bachelard calls resonance (*résonance*), the plane of our existence in the world, our personal associations to the portrayed world (memories, affects, etc.), and reverberation (*retentissement*), an ontological plane of discovery in which we become aware of certain possibilities of our being as the foundation of these responses.[9] Thus the reader's role in reverie has a double aspect. As the experience of the archetypal imaginary is incorporated into the familiar, this process happens also to bring about a *virement d'être*, a swerve in being, which reveals imaginative possibilities that pervade human existence, offering transcendence. Thus reverie satisfies our recessive desires to know and linger in a fantastic world and at the same time provides the possibility for a critique of the real.

In the experience of the imaginary, once reverie has awakened it, the image reaches down into the roots of our existence, touching and activating the dynamic material archetypes of the collective unconscious, leaving this realm to soar upwards in flights of sublimation that are expansions, not dispersals of being. A fantastic world discovered through reverie may involve many doublings of the self, and even the entire sequence of individuation according to Jung (anima, persona, shadow, Wise Old Man etc.) may be staged, but in its pure form reverie is never demonic. Or apocalyptic. In reverie the dreaming self is always present and capable of piloting its activities which mediate between the conscious and unconscious realms of the psyche. The image for Bachelard is a plenitude which always fills the dreamer's space. And, as we have mentioned before, reverie at its most expressive moment becomes endowed with cosmic significance:

> Faced with this extravagance of fruits which invites us to taste the world, faced with the World-Fruits which solicit our reveries, how is it possible not to affirm that the man of reverie is cosmically happy. A type of happiness corresponds to each image. You cannot say

of the man of reverie that he is "thrown to the world." For him the world is all welcome, and he himself is the principle of welcome. The man of reverie bathes in the happiness of dreaming the world, bathes in the well-being of a happy world.[10]

In a fantasy text based purely on reverie, the reader would have the double consciousness of his own well-being and of a happy world. The man of reverie and the world of being would be interrelated on the same level of being. It should be pointed out that the Bachelard finds this experience of pure reverie most often in poetry, and in the passage quoted above his archetypal pronouncements are being made with reference to a poem by Rilke entitled "Dancing the Orange" (*Tanzt die Orange*). In narrative texts this happiness is sometimes achieved only with difficulty. In discussing them Bachelard was concerned always to point out instances of unhappy fixation in reading which he studied under the sign "culture complex."

According to Maurice Merleau-Ponty, the unconscious complex can be understood phenomenologically as a separated dialectic of consciousness, a mental automaton gifted with an internal logic, that behaves as an acquired and durable structure of consciousness with regard to a category of stimuli.[11] The complex points to a psychic integration that has been achieved only in appearance and which leaves certain relatively isolated systems in effect which the subject refuses to transform and assume. Bachelard clearly has something very like this in mind for the culture complex which allows for the possibility of a fragmented life of consciousness, because in *The Psychoanalysis of Fire* he posits an "alert dialectics" of sublimation that would allow the reader/dreamer to liberate happy reverie.[12] In the last analysis, says Bachelard, all the complexes attached to the imaginative experience of fire are fragmented, painful. They limit our desire in the moment of fulfilling it. To seize fire or to give oneself to the flames, to annihilate or to be annihilated, to follow the Prometheus complex or the Empedocles complex, is both conducive to the writing of poetry and the acquiring of neurosis. What is needed for the poetic imagination is a means of transforming these negative mental automatons "in the very precise sense of C. G. Jung."[13]

Bachelardian reverie thus has many affinities with Jungian fantasy, and especially with the idea, foremost in Jung, that the unconscious provides compensation in the form of archetypal figures for deficiencies in the conscious outlook. Indeed, in the process of Jungian analysis, the subject is encouraged to assimilate hints or fragments of unconscious complexes and, by associating them with parallel elements, to elaborate them in clearly visual form. Jungian active fantasy overcomes in this manner dissociated psychic states with the positive participation of consciousness.[14] Likewise, according to Bachelard, literary reverie always allows for the participation of a conscious self in the shaping of its released spontaneity, unlike the nocturnal dream which remains antithetical to consciousness. Bachelard then does not share the Freudian view of culture which argues that it requires massive repression and continued sublimation to maintain itself above the instinctual level. Using a botanical metaphor, he says that he seeks man above the graft, where "culture has put its mark on nature."[f]

Thus it is by their cultural signs that Bachelard identifies the complexes—Novalis, Ophelia, Prometheus—and identifies them as orientations of the educated reader. As I mentioned in the introduction, little purpose would be served by discussing these structures for themselves. The reader will find an account of the complex in question provided with the analysis of each story. They can be useful designations of a fusion between natural dreams and acquired traditions, if one wanted to study them as part of a thematology. I intend them to function, however, on the level of Iser's heuristic model of the implied reader, that is, as part of the text's structural repertoire. As such, they provide a familiar framework within which to study the production of structured acts of consciousness that constitute a fantasy world.

With respect to the reading process, we might say that during reading we locate and activate a certain complex, perhaps through identification with a character. In some cases we may even say that complex *is* character, insofar as it is a center of conscious orientation in a story.[16] This complex is capable of embodying and evoking whole realms of social norms and cultural conventions. On a less conscious level, in terms of the production of passive syntheses, it directs the reading process by assembling images into organized constellations that are the beginnings of our experience of the imaginary. Particular images may be spaced out thematically along the narrative during the time-flow of reading, but the familiar complex enables us to draw everything towards a center. Temporarily, therefore, the complex may give the work an inner cohesiveness and stability from one point of view. In this way, it aids the reader in the process of consistency-building. The reader assumes the reading complex which then guides the further production of passive syntheses.

But if there are several complexes, or strategies which set up a conflict with or undermine familiar complexes, antagonistic effects are produced together with the drive to resolve them. This may be the source of the experience Northrop Frye records when he says that the romancer, as opposed to the novelist, deals with characters that are "idealized by revery, and however conservative he may be, something nihilistic and untamable is likely to keep breaking out of his pages."[17] In any case the reader has then to imaginatively transform the complex he has taken over from the text. This in turn leads to self-discovery, putting the reader in touch with the sublimation of archetypal realities which underlie the complex. As we read through the text in a linear way, moving outward to cultural references, the text's familiar norms and codifications of the world, we are also drawn inwards to the discovery of reverie, and the emergence of the oneiric level of the text constitutes for us the transcendence of these fragmented perspectives.

Summarizing the typical trajectory of our aesthetic response to reverie, we may say that first isolated material images stimulate our daydream faculty of mind, reverie, which then awakens subliminally our desire to "penetrate" further into this world, to imagine it further. Complexes, either of narrator or character, organize the production of these passive syntheses, enabling us to prolong and metamorphose these images in a process of anticipation and recollection guided by the text. Soon we become conscious of a transformation going on in ourselves in which we realize our desire for a cosmic happiness. In the utopian novel this experience of the imaginary may give rise to social criticism, and it is in this manner that reverie becomes cognitive, as I show in a later chapter, but here it is the sublimative reader's need for idealization that needs to be clarified:

> Of course, culture complexes are grafted upon the deeper complexes which have been brought to light by psychoanalysis. As Charles Baudouin has emphasized, a complex is essentially a psychic transformer. The culture complex continues this transformation: cultural sublimation prolongs natural sublimation. To the cultivated man, a sublimated image never seems beautiful enough; he would like to renew the sublimation. If sublimation were simply a matter of concepts, it would stop as soon as the image is enclosed within conceptual lines. But color overflows, matter multiplies, images develop; dreams keep their impetus despite the poems expressing them.[18]

This notion of readerly sublimation differs considerably from most psychoanalytic theories of reading, for example, Norman N. Holland's. In Holland's development of Freudian theory, sublimation is a movement towards intellectual understanding of the text, and a desexualization which allows disguised and partial satisfaction of an unconscious core fantasy so that the reader's ego can "make sense" of his reading experience. But surprisingly sublimation is not, according to Holland, a defense mechanism analogous to the formal properties of the literary work which enable us to master the turbulence of an awakened fantasy, since it operates, Holland says, not so much against the presence of fantasy material as with it in what he calls the press towards theme.[19] It is therefore the essence of those "changes and disguises," those substitutions of the Freudian aesthetic, which provide the means by which the artist hides the egotistical nature of his fantasy from the public (and through which the reader escapes his own censor, the superego).

Yet Holland's reader is not really sublimative in Bachelard's sense, for the underlying fantasy is archetypal and Jungian in Bachelard, Freudian and personal in Holland. Holland's reader is one who introjects the text, one who makes of it a subsystem of his ego, managing and transforming its nuclear fantasy towards meaningfulness; Bachelard's reader has no apparent need to master anything with intellectual meaning. Holland argues that in this transformational process by which we come to feel the text as part of our own mental activity, we analogize, enriching the central fantasy with our own associations and experiences that relate to it. It is this process of analogizing that Holland finds in Bachelard's texts. He says that a Bachelardian reading helps the reader in his fusion with the work, and this may certainly be true for the resonance aspect of reverie. But Bachelardian sublimation is not based on a prior incorporation of the text. (Holland's reader is really an introjective, not sublimative reader.) On the contrary, the experience of the imaginary has first to be built up through the process of consistency-building, and material imagination. Especially material imagination, which "overflows" conceptual schemas. Therefore if Bachelard argues that the reader experiences in reverie a fusion with the world of childhood imagination, that fusion is anything but repressed or disguised; it is an ontological discovery of our being.

Material imagination refers us to that realm of valued objects discovered in childhood that are not just disguised substitutions for unconsciously desired objects defined by lack and Oedipal triangularity (the phallus, the breast), but the very expression of our existential situation in a world of natural productive forces: "the *free material region*, these objects which have not received social interdictions."[20] Sublimation is consequently not a response to lack, but to excess, beautiful plentitude. As Bachelard says in the passage quoted above, if sublimation were simply a matter of concepts, it would stop as soon as images were enclosed within conceptual lines. But in fantasy based on material images, color overflows the boundaries of form, matter multiplies, images flower and develop in the reader's mind revealing his poetic being.

Bachelard criticizes the Freudian notion of continuous sublimation with the notion of a dialectical sublimation that moves away from conceptualizations towards an erotization of the body into aesthetic sensuousness. Sublimation is not, for Bachelard, a "normal" desexualization that somehow avoids repression of the sexual instincts by transforming aim and object. Rather, reverie draws upon idealized figures of the collective unconscious as alternative existential relations to reality. Bachelard therefore speaks of sublimation as a movement towards the ideal. Imagination effects a break with instinctual realities and transforms them towards higher, cultural values, and is the true source of psychic limits: ". . . it is the reverie which delineates the furthest limits of our mind."[21] Cultural sublimations (reading/writing) are in Bachelard's view part of a dialectical process in which an instinctual impulse is cancelled or subdued, but then given a different direction, liberated and transformed all without the help of concepts.

Which is not to say that reverie does not give rise to cognition. Returning our discussion now to the structured aspects of the repertoire, we may say that if character is complex, then an archetype may be conceived of as a structure that bears all potential realizations within itself and provides the basis for all its subsequent variations. This usage is similar to that of Northrop Frye, who understands archetypes as structural principles of storytelling that define the world of our desires. In the introduction to the English translation of *The Psychoanalysis of Fire,* Frye in fact tries to arrange Bachelard's culture complexes into his schema of archetypal imagery which, although it does have a strong Jungian bias, is nevertheless still an Aristotelian description of plot as shape or arrangement of action. This is certainly a useful and rational attempt to systematize Bachelard's reflections on literature. We should be aware, however, of what we would lose from this assimilation, because the world of mythical imagery in Frye is really an abstract, static pattern of meaning which he assumes the reader to find at some moment of convergence in the reading process. In terms of narrative, myth is "the imitation of actions near or at the conceivable limits of desire," but in terms of meaning (which Frye apparently thinks exists in the text apart from any reader's interaction with it), myth is "the same world looked at as an area or field of activity. . . the meaning or pattern of poetry is a structure of imagery with conceptual implications."[22]

Now, we have just seen that if images begin to have conceptual implications for Bachelard, he rejects them as artificial and imitative, not strong enough to materialize the fantastic. But how, then, do the sublimative images of fantasy become cognitive in Bachelardian reverie? It is not my intention here to reconcile the "two Bachelards," the man of science and the man of reverie, the diurnal man and the nocturnal man. Perhaps only surrealism can accomplish such a task.[23] Undoubtedly Bachelard would have scoffed at such a notion as *science* fiction, since for him literature is the site of desire, which must be actively and even puritanically repressed in scientific endeavors. Indeed, *The Psychoanalysis of Fire* is mostly an exposé of the affective distortions of knowledge that can be found in supposedly scientific accounts of this phenomena. Much of the irony of that book lies in its juxtaposition of supposedly scientific texts with literary reverie about fire. However, literature in his view was related to science in the sense that it provides a necessary correction to the extremes of the scientific mind which requires such a break with the function of inhabiting a world.

Fantasy literature at its best (of which I trust there are some examples in this study) is an appeal to the total person and a special refreshment of our humanity. It should therefore be studied as an emotive-cognitive synthesis. To argue that it makes an appeal only to irrationalism and consequently should be dismissed outright, as Suvin seems to do, is ultimately to take sides with irrationalism, to demarcate emotion, like religion and art, from everything deserving the title of knowledge or cognition. Under cover of this enmity emotion and human expression, even culture as a whole, are withdrawn from thought.

It is this point which it seems to me is made so brilliantly by Herbert Marcuse in his *Eros and Civilization* (1955). Marcuse argues that the cognitive value of reverie lies in its preservation of a non-alienated relation to nature.[24] Fantasy (and Marcuse is thinking primarily of Freudian fantasy) does not accept as final the limitations imposed on freedom and happiness by the domination of repressive reason. Marcuse calls this aspect of fantasy the Great Refusal, and draws several times on Bachelard's writings to show us what the experience of this unrepressed aesthetic sensuousness of the total person would be like.[25] In the figures of

Orpheus and Narcissus are preserved a world of beauty and overflowing plenitude of being, a sphere outside labor and toil (the performance principle). It is the poet's day-dreaming allegiance to the pleasure principle and childhood reverie which constitutes their dialectical truth values: play and display, the gratification and released potentialities of both man and nature.

I intend to show in later chapters that Bradbury is making use of reverie for the same cognitive (and sublimative) purposes. His fantasy offers us the pleasures of participation in the recreative dialectics we have outlined above.

3

Reverie and the Marvelous

In this chapter and the next we will examine two of Bradbury's early attempts at fantasy in the marvelous and Gothic traditions. I am not so much interested in linking them to these traditions as examples of it as I am in showing how reverie is present as a softening and transforming influence. The first story contains an object reverie and the second an exploration of the splittings and doublings that accompany the *anima-animus dialectic* of reverie. A typical object reverie involves a fathoming of the object in its material intimacy which then offers us a world. Most of us have had the experience of the revelation of a marvelous interior by certain objects: one discovers flowers and figures in the intimacy of frost or crystal, a play of sculpture and design in stone. The object reverie typically goes in a multiple trajectory from exterior to interior, from interior to exterior. Among the objects which privilege this sort of dynamic dreaming consciousness are of course sea shells, and our first story is about the discovery of a fantastic world through inhabiting one. The doublings of the self in reverie are characteristically less harsh and demonic than those of the Gothic, reverie itself being dominated by images of feminine repose. Our second story involves a fantastic world imagined by a woman frustrated by and afraid of her lover in the real world, though she is nonetheless a prodigious dreamer of mutual idealization.

It is no accident that both stories take place on occasions ideal for reverie and reading itself in the real world - vacations, periods of recuperation from illness, and lazy, rainy afternoons. In these early stories Bradbury is exploring his strategy for reverie which will later culminate in *The Martian Chronicles* and *Fahrenheit 451* where a whole kaleidoscopic array of reveries is presented to the reader. These novels are in themselves largely self-contained fantasy worlds, not marked by transitions from the ordinary to the fantastic (though it could be argued that *Fahrenheit 451* moves from a fantastic world to a real one). In any case the modern fantastic, as written by Bradbury, does not merely involve the laying bare of Gothic props and supernatural conventions. As always with Bradbury's poetics of reverie, it is a question of having the reader respond to a world and it is this which must be studied.

"The Sea Shell" (1944) was first published in the pulp magazine *Weird Tales*, of interest now because it introduced us to so many American authors of weird and horror fiction: H. P. Lovecraft, Robert Bloch, Clark Ashton Smith, and Bradbury himself, to name just a few.[1] It is one of Bradbury's earliest stories exploring childhood and reverie, creating both suspense and surprise as part of its overall discovery-structure. Because of the typical trajectory of this discovery-structure, "The Sea Shell" is practically an allegory of the reader's task in texts based on reverie and consequently we will want to examine it in some detail. It also contains one of the essential themes of the self in nineteenth-century fantastic literature according to Tzvetan Todorov: metamorphosis or rebirth to another self.[2]

Readers aware of the Romantic tradition will perhaps already have in mind from the title Wordsworth's poetic dream in the fifth book of *The Prelude*. As W. H. Auden points out in his archetypal poetic mediation on this dream of Wordsworth, *The Enchafèd Flood,* the siren voice of the poetic shell calls men to the sea, the double kingdom, to put off their human nature and be trolls.[3] This prospect is alluring to the child in our story (and a rebirth motif is very much in evidence, though subtly handled), but he is not faced with the adult dilemma of the romantic hero according to Auden, which is the danger of becoming through this transformation a purely self-conscious ego. His problem is really the essential problem of adolescence, "that fever of time in human life," as Bachelard says.[4] Initially, his impatience appears to be due to an inability to sublimate in the Freudian manner, deferring his immediate desires with the substitution of another, more socially acceptable object. But actually the sublimation involved is that of reverie for the object does not give rise only to intellectual constructs. It gives rise to a fantastic world. We may call this problem the Omar Khayyam complex, since it is brought out consciously by the boy's mother and therefore the adult perspective, as such. She manifests a wistful kind of sadness towards him, no doubt because she knows what the adult world will do to her boy's dreams. In terms of oneiric criticism, she becomes a kind of anima figure (a feminine character who transmits the reverie object, or helps the reader/dreamer discover his own capacity for reverie, and guides him in that process) as she transmits the reverie object to her son, which provides the means for his escape.

"The Sea Shell" is an allegory of reverie and the reading process because the child's fidelity to the sea shell (often a symbol of psychic transformation and therefore familiar ground in the repertoire) and his persistent day-dreaming of it during his convalescence, allows him to transcend the boredom of his harassed confinement in an act of pure transcendence and flight from the real world. As it turns out, the reader himself has to imagine through a surprise ending how this transcendence came about, but it is nevertheless subliminally prepared for him in descriptions of the child's inner world given by the narrator. In terms of oneiric criticism, this surprise has a later integrative phase, that of Bachelardian reverberation, in which the surprising aspects are seen in connection with what has gone before, with the whole drift of reading experience. In short the reader is brought to a confrontation with his own constitutive activity.

In this manner a dynamic dialectic of inside and out, of familiar and unfamilar, is generated by the spirals of the reverie object. Primarily we see things from the child's limited point of view. That the child may be carried *too* far away is certainly suggested, since the alluring voices that come from the shell seem to anticipate his reactions. Some readers may feel uneasy about the prospect of the child being trapped in a world so different from that of an adult, but this reaction stems from our sharing of the mother's point of view. Bradbury's basic strategy is to present through a fantastic event the inadequacy of our adult view of things. This in turn releases the reader's spontaneity to seek a deeper understanding of the relationship between childhood imagination and reality.

The plot which underlies this transformation is realistic and straightforward, concerned with the everyday activities of parents and children in the midst of warm domesticity. We are surrounded by what is obviously an American small-town landscape. Johnny Bishop is an eleven-year-old who is simply too impatient to wait a week for his cold to take its natural course. He wants to be out of bed, and outside to play pirate with his friends. The action of the Omar Khayyam complex organizes for the reader all those images and suggestions of compulsive hurrying that appear in the time-flow of reading. The norms of the adult world, the world of constraints on desire and deferral of satisfaction, are represented in the text by the mother. She gives her son a sea shell "to have fun with," hoping that it will ease his impatience. But this only leads to more questions on the part of the boy. The mother finds that she cannot frame an answer to his naive questions about the value of these deferrals. In this manner two very different perspectives are set in a hermeneutic tension and revolve around the sea shell. In the solitude and repose during the next day and night, Johnny begins to inhabit the world of the shell, by listening to the sounds of the imaginary ocean contained in it. This landscape comes more and more to dominate the real world, until supernatural voices beckon the boy to come away. Finally the mother discovers that Johnny is not in his room, and, thinking that he has disobeyed her in running off to play with his friends, she picks up the shell. She hears Johnny playing in the surf when she puts it to her ear.

Having discussed the repertoire and strategies of this text, we can now proceed to treat it as an allegory of our theory of reading. It should be stressed for the sake of clarity however that in general and in all cases where we are dealing with imagistic acts of consciousness produced from a text, to objectivate does not mean to reify. I am simply thematizing and bringing out for analysis those acts of consciousness which were operative in passive syntheses during reading in order to reveal how the process of consistency-building is built up and destroyed, giving rise to the experience of the imaginary and the reader's released spontaneity. Those acts of consciousness described remain dynamic and functional for other readers. Since the story is short, I will quote extensively from it in order to give the reader the all-important sense of context within which reverie develops. It begins by formulating a desire:

> He wanted to get out and run, bounding over hedges, kicking tin cans down the alley, shouting at all the windows for the gang to come and play. The sun was up and the day was bright, and here he was swaddled with bed clothes, sweating and scowling, and not liking it at all. (p. 388)

As we are made familiar with the world of this story in this opening paragraph, we can already sense the presence of a self (or complex) in a childhood landscape and certain magical acts, emotive images, relating to that landscape. There are, in fact, two opposing landscapes that can be observed on closer inspection. One is imaginary and desired, the other is real and frustrating. Thus a subliminal suspense, a tension of inside and out, is generated at the outset. The landscape of activity the boy desires is outside; to escape to it he transforms the frustrating situation inside by recourse to imaginary acts (which are also emotive intentions) that evoke the presence of objects from that desired landscape: an alley, tin cans to kick, windows to shout at, friends to play with. The objects are given as having value within the horizon of his imaginary play on this sunny, bright day. In the imaginary landscape the boy can move freely, without resistance from the pragmatic world. The real world reveals itself as confining, and the boy is "not liking it at all."

The swaddling clothes, objects which resist his activity, also hint at the rebirth motif and at the fact that for the moment he is a helpless baby, a prospect at which he scowls. Because the situation is difficult and he has no means of escape as yet, the boy has unreflectively invested the world with frustration and is living it as such. The swaddling clothes *are* his sweating confinement. It is the world which appears frustrating. However, by an emotional and magical act negating his situation, the boy has also made imaginatively present to us another landscape. There is a strong subliminal link here with the body as landscape. As we shall see, the boy will act on his own sublimatory "lost" body in reverie in order to escape this frustrating situation (in the real world, the fever effectively separates him from his body, makes him self-conscious of it).

The story continues to present more familiar objects of the inside convalescent world subtly transformed by the child's imagination: perfumes (his mother's, orange juice and medicine) evoke the presence of objects that have passed through the atmosphere and are now absent. This scent-laden atmosphere is expressive of a passive mind saturated with emotion and memory, against which the boy rebels. The day is "up," and a shaft or sunlight strikes *down* at him. The patch-work quilt appears to shout at him, just as he imagines shouting at the windows outside. Objects of this world magically shout back at him:

> The entire lower half of the patch-work quilt was a circus banner of red, green, purple
> and blue. It practically yelled color into his eyes. Johnny fidgeted
>   "I wanna go out," he complained softly. "Darn it. Darn it." A fly buzzed, bumping
> again and again at the window pane with a dry staccato of its transparent wings.
>   Johnny looked at it, understanding how it wanted out, too. (p. 288)

A circus is a world of brightly clashing colors which creates at times the magical illusion of flying apart. A multi-colored banner rippling in the wind and sun is its metonymic emblem. The important thing about this emblem (besides the formal tension of its colors) is, phenomenologically, the implied spatial structure which is operative here. The banner is always placed at the top of a pole or mast, overlooking the circus world. The raised position of the banner literally expresses ex-*alta*tion, or the desire to heighten one's life by raising it above the normal level (sublimation in the Bachelardian sense). Generally, a banner is a sign of victory or self-assertion, but poor Johnny seems wrapped in a defeat which yells color at his eyes. He finds an equivalent for his situation in a not-so-antiseptic creature that normally belongs to the outside world also. The fly "shouts" against the window with its transparent wings that suggest magical flight. As we are made familiar with these objects (the window, the bed-quilt, etc.) we also take over these subliminal, emotive image-structures which appear transformed subtly again in the following sequences (especially the last, where they serve to ground the familiar world which is then abruptly transformed, and through an object with which we are going to be made very familiar: the sea shell).

The mother brings Johnny the bad news that he will have to remain in bed for another two days, a fact that arouses his consternation. He resents having to drink more "healthful" fluids, even if the taste is disguised with orange juice, but the mother offers no medicine this time, only an unfamiliar object:

> "This time—no medicine."
> "What's that in your hand?"
> "Oh, this?" Mother held out a round, spiralled gleaming object.
>   Johnny took it. It was hard and shiny and—pretty. "Doctor Hull dropped by a few
> minutes ago and left it. He thought you might have fun with it." (p. 389)

It should be pointed out that the mother emerges into this conversation from a freshly polished hall shining from the care with which she has touched it. The house is her reverie object, and although she is an adult, as anima figure she still has the sensuous feel for objects that awakens reverie. There is a subliminal suggestion that the boy is already living within a polished shell. Be that as it may, we now find emerging here a network of intentionality surrounding the shell. The doctor sends it as an object intended to be healthful and to assuage the boy's impatience. For her part, the mother transmits these values and shows the boy how to imagine the shell in the next sequence. Because she is an adult, however, she does not transform the shell into a world, although she certainly invests it with value (perhaps she thinks of it as a distraction for her son). Her affective grasp of this object is therefore weak or delicate when compared to the boy's surprise.

The irony is, of course, that the boy will do more than just "have fun" with the shell in rejecting the norms of the adult world. The child will become so familiar with the gift that he genuinely surprises his mother (and us) at the end. He will transform his "Omar Khayyam complex" by living it completely, by transcending it towards a childhood world without parental complexes. For the moment, however, let us note that the shell forms the center of a developing narrative network embracing all the characters. Johnny's first perception of the inanimate shell is from the outside; it is seen as having a humanly-defined lure of prettiness whose resistant textures (hard and shiny and spiralled) invite a loving caress. But the boy is dubious, perhaps because the object *is* unfamiliar, and he needs to classify it before he will accept it:

> Johnny looked palely dubious. His small hands brushed the slick surface. "How can I have fun with it? I don't even know what it is!"
> Mother's smile was better than sunshine. "It's a shell from the sea, Johnny. Doctor Hull picked it up on the Pacific shore last year when he was out there."
> "Hey, that's all right. What kind of shell is it?"
> "Oh, I don't know. Some form of sea life probably lived in it once, a long time ago."
> Johnny's brows went up. "Lived in this? Made it a home?"
> "Yes."
> "Aw—really?"
> She adjusted it in his hand. "If you don't believe me, listen for yourself, young man. Put this end—here—against your ear."
> "Like this?" He raised the shell to his small pink ear and pressed it tight. "Now what do I do?"
> Mother smiled. "Now, if you're very quiet, and listen closely, you'll hear something very, very familiar."
> Johnny listened. His ear opened imperceptibly like a small flower opening, waiting.
> A titanic wave came in on a rocky shore and smashed itself down.
> "The sea!" cried Johnny Bishop. "Oh, Mom! The ocean! The waves! The sea!"
> Wave after wave came in on that distant, craggy shore. Johnny closed his eyes tight black and a smile folded his small face exactly in half. Wave after pounding wave roared in his small pinkly alert ear.
> "Yes, Johnny," said Mother. "The sea." (p. 389)

Another landscape (still distant because the child is not immersed in it as yet) has been made imaginatively present. The mother's magic (the magic of the Other in transforming *my* world) is to transform Johnny's world from the outside.[5] She shows him the very familiar in the unfamiliar, teaching him to discover the marvelous by patient listening to the reverberation of images (Bachelard's *retentissement*). The sea shell is indeed a marvelous reverie object because it contains within it an intimate immensity—the boy can hold the ocean in the palm of his hand. At the beginning of this passage the shell is somewhat of an empty schema for the child. He has no knowledge of it other than what is given in perception or from his mother who guides him through this reverie experience. He is given some knowledge of it from her (she tells him it is from the Pacific shore) which he then fills in with affective intentions in order to transform his situation. The shell is first hypothesized as containing life (the waves have the activity and weight of bodies here)—which the child initially disputes. The boy is dubious about any living creature wanting to live in such a confined space. But then he is asked to listen (imagine for himself) in order to discover that life. He discovers to his surprise the internal landscape of the sea within it. Magically, the sea shell works a kind of spell on him. Coming from the Other, and yet being safe, it shatters the pragmatic order of the day by disrupting his expectations.

But Johnny also acts unreflectively on himself. He "lives" this illusion in which the world seems changed. He is able to inhabit this magical world in an instant, through the phenomenon of belief created by the incantation of the waves pounding on the beach. Now, these imaginative acts are already a transformation of the world which has become too difficult for him. They are the means by which he apprehends this new and unfamiliar object. Imagination in reverie is therefore not merely the filling in of empty schemas of knowledge with images. It is also the magical emotive transformation of those objects as we would like them to be (and just for the sake of oneiric verisimilitude, Bradbury has us learn in the next section that the boy has never *seen* the ocean but is working from analogies of a local lake by exaggerating images. Exaggeration, according to Bachelard, is the surest sign of wonder).

Normally, we learn about new objects through perception, that is, by *degrees.* They offer solid resistance to our attempts to know them; they are never (or rarely) seen as totalities, only as given in perspective, in facets. In fact the boy expresses his *impatience* with this perceptual process. How can I have fun with it, he says, if I don't know what it is, as if only those things which offer instantaneously the promise of a world (namely, images) are worthy enough to hold a world of freedom. The mother hopes to teach the boy patience by listening, but we can see that he has discovered that reverie negates a problematic world of frustration and setbacks (the adult world) by offering an instantaneous transformation in which we "live" our desires. And it must be persistently believed in , dreamt with fidelity, if it is to rival the real world. As we shall see, that is exactly what Johnny does in the following sequences.

But what of the reader's role thus far? Has his capacity for reverie been activated? Bachelard himself was extremely fond of shells, but he points out in *The Poetics of Space,* where he devotes an entire chapter to them, that the material imagination suffers a kind of defeat before this beautifully formal object. For Bachelard the shell would seem a triumph of the formal imagination, nature herself having dreamt pure geometry in a spiral that nevertheless represents the life force itself. How is it possible, Bachelard wonders, to surpass nature in her own dream? Perhaps, Bachelard suggests, we should begin phenomenologically with the naive observer, the child, before the object which will invite his daydream. Now, because the shell is a hollow object that once contained life, it has borne the traditional associations of the allegory of body and soul. In order to avoid these scholarly accretions therefore what one needs to consider is the "function of inhabiting" these objects. This will counter the classifying tendencies of the conchologist.

Then, says Bachelard, a lively dialectics of childhood wonderment emerges. In the textual play of his own meditation Bachelard considers many descriptions of melusines and fantastic monsters that dreamers have imagined to inhabit empty shells. He comments on fantastic texts where wondrously large creatures, like elephants, emerge from small shells, activating a dialectics of large and small. The phenomenologist's imagination is also stimulated by the dialectics of creatures that are free and others that are in fetters. Bachelard notes however that this exercise often leads to a fear-curiosity complex. We want to see what is in the shell, but we are afraid of what might leap out at us:

> These undulations of fear and curiosity increase when reality is not there to moderate them, that is, when we are imagining. However, let's not invent, but rather give documents concerning images which have actually been imagined or drawn, and which have remained engraved in precious and other stones. There is a passage in the book by Jurgis Baltrusaitis in which he recalls the *action* of an artist who shows a dog that "leaps from its shell" and pounces upon a rabbit. One degree more of aggressiveness and the shell-dog would attack a man. This is a clear example of the progressing type of action by means of which imagination surpasses reality. For here the imagination acts upon not only geometrical dimensions, but upon elements of power and speed as well—not in an enlarged space, either, but in a more rapid tempo. When the motion picture camera accelerates the unfolding of a flower, we receive a sublime image of offering; it is as though the flower we see opening so quickly and without reservation, sensed the meaning of a gift; as though it were a gift from the world. But if the cinema showed us a snail emerging from its shell in fast motion, or pushing its horns toward the sky very rapidly, what an aggression that would be! What aggressive horns! All our curiosity would be blocked by fear, and the fear-curiosity complex would be torn apart.[6]

It should now be apparent that we have not been wandering from our topic, the reader's role, as might first have seemed. The undulating spiral of fear and curiosity is not allowed to increase (as yet) because reality *is* there in our story in the form of a generalized schema of a shell to moderate it. The mother is guiding the reader as well, by assuring him that Johnny is going to find something very very familiar in the shell. We are assured that no fantastic animal is going to suddenly leap upon us—as perhaps would happen in some weird or horror stories. Our imagination is not allowed aggressively to surpass reality.

Furthermore, the fear aspect of this reading complex is softened by the narrator's flower image, which offers to the reader the promise of a safe refuge in inhabiting the shell. We can describe phenomenologically how this feeling is established for the reader by passive syntheses in the following manner. The reader has first of all to build up a series of equivalences between flower and shell. A flower is a formal image, equivalent to a shell in that respect, but unlike the shell it is rapidly opening, suggesting a certain dynamism. An open image is the only image sure to bring about reverie. Second, Johnny's ear opens imperceptibly. We are not asked to perceive, but to imagine a small flower opening, waiting. The flower image is not just a static metaphor, but suggests an equivalent to Johnny's experience which is in the nature of a guarded, protected opening to an as yet strange and unfamiliar world. The reader's further imagination of Johnny's ear as another kind of shell, small and pink, is thus mediated by an oneiric image, hence its central position in this passage.

Thus the oneiric level of the text aids us imperceptibly in integrating two dimensions of experience, self and world. The flower image presents the reader with interiority that invites intimacy; it gives him the assurance that he is going to link up oneiric relations that reverie will make inexhaustible in this new world. In short, the flower defines the reader's imaginative position in an instantaneous act of consciousness: the reader is centered as in the center of a flower, surrounded by rays of color in the delicately nuanced petals of meaning. And if we now consider Bachelard's fantasy about the rapidly opening flower, then this surprise image of offering can be linked back oneirically to the doctor's and the mother's gifts. This surprise linking introduces an oneiric level of significance to narrative consciousness, tells us that the reverie world offers itself as a flower to us, and assures us that we will inhabit this world without fear.

At the end of this sequence, when the waves wash refreshingly again and again over it, Johnny's ear is practically a small pink creature inhabiting the shell. If he is then a creature "in fetters" in the large shell of the house, then one definitely gets the feeling that he is going to prepare this small space as a means of dynamic escape. His ear is now "pinkly alert," that is, now that the equivalence of the house and shell have been established by an oneiric logic of invention (if the entire sea can be contained in such a small space, why not a boy?). Johnny closes his eyes "tight black," smiling broadly, no longer wanting to consider the shell in formal imagination. No longer respecting form or color (those stable things) he is seized by a conviction of a refuge in which life can be concentrated and then transcended by leaping to meet the in-coming waves.

Let us now summarize the passive syntheses that we have made thematic in the past few pages. Initially, the boy is seduced by the unfamiliar formal and sensuous beauty of the shell. He wants to classify it in order to play with it in an exterior fashion. This is as far a Freudian sublimation would go—the limit of the concept. The shell is then hypothesized as containing life, but the boy is dubious about any creature wanting to inhabit such a small space. It seems a very small and confining world indeed. The mother/anima figure then guides the boy by putting the shell to his ear so that he can "believe" in the statement she has made. Then, as we have seen, this gesture activates the fantasy of rebirth to another world. Johnny finally leaves behind the formal imagination (which, as Bachelard says, defeats the production of images) and establishes an imaginative grounding in *matter,* the water which will underlie and sustain the play of surface imagery in the third sequence. Johnny can hear the play of his friends outside:

> Their voices seemed so far away, lazy, drifting on a tide of sun. The sunlight was just like deep yellow, lambent water, lapping at the summer, full tide. Slow, languorous, warm, lazy. The whole world was over its head in that tide and everything was slowed down. The clock ticked slower. The street car came down the avenue in warm metal slow motion. It was almost like seeing a motion film that is losing speed and noise. Everything was softer. Nothing seemed to count as much.
>
> He wanted to get out and play, badly. He kept watching the kids climbing the fences, playing soft ball, roller skating in the warm languor. His head felt heavy, heavy, heavy. His eyelids were window sashes pulling down, down. The sea shell lay against his ear. He pressed it close.
>
> Pounding, drumming, waves broke on a shore. A yellow sand shore. And when the waves went back out they left foam, like the suds of beer, on the sand. The suds broke and vanished, like dreams. And more waves came with more foam. And the sand crabs tumbled, salt-wet, scuttling brown, in the ripples. Cool green water pounding on the sand. The very sound of it conjured up visions; the ocean breeze soothed Johnny Bishop's small body. Suddenly the hot afternoon was no longer hot and depressing. The clock started ticking faster. The street cars clanged metal quickly. The slowness of the summer world was spanked into crisp life by the pound-pound of waves on an unseen and brilliant beach. (p. 390)

Insofar as I have been able to determine, this is the earliest example in Bradbury's fantasy of a deliberately narrated daydream. As such, it is an exemplary illustration of a dreaming subject going into image-making reverie in an imaginary landscape unseen yet brilliant. It unfolds in three phases which are coherent deformations of each other. The dozing style of the first phase seems to me to evoke the mingling of memory and imagination. It suggests long solitary hours spent lying idle on the beach at Fox Lake, where we know the boy has vacationed before. It is the recollection of a real landscape of gently lapping water that gradually immerses the real world with the help of the boy's imagination. Once he finds this element he wants to develop it further, to sublimate it further from small lake to ocean. As the boy half shuts his eyes in the lazy warmth, the two landscapes, real and imagined, seem to melt into each other. The world seems bathed in the languorous yellow light of this remembered daydream; indeed, it appears to be underwater (suggesting the pastness of the past), and objects of the familiar outside world are being slowed down by the resistance of the tide of liquid sun. Notice especially the "far away" perception of objects that are softened by reverie into meaning less than they normally do as utensils in the real world. The metal of the street car is on the verge of a surreal deformation.

The same phenomenological psychology that was operative before is again operative here—he finds the world difficult and tries to escape, this time by falling back into a reverie he had experienced long ago, one which has been reactivated by his discovery of the sea shell's reverberating interiority. It is thus the reverie object which activates the archetype of watery rebirth, but I am not arguing for any causal determinism here. The real world in fact appears to be losing speed and time—and its grip on him. No doubt the boy has something of a fever, but convalescence here is simply a metaphor for reverie (in one of his aphorisms Bachelard asks us: is not every convalescence a childhood?). The body is again the substratum for reverie. The text gives us a humorous comparison of the boy's eyes closing like window sashes shutting out the unreachable desired world of play outside. It is a familiar enough metaphor, but appropriate to the hypnagogic phases of reverie where acts of consciousness may take on a dramatized form. Of course the whole point of the metaphor is to show us that the boy does not *want* to fall asleep where he would be something less than an active subject pursuing his own intentions.

The only recourse is to evoke a world of activity, and when the boy puts the shell to his ear in the second phase, we enter reverie proper. The beach is described as an independent world, as brilliant yet unseen. No transition is given by the narrator; the world is magically *there*, rivalling the real world through the incantation of its waves. The shell recalls the yellow sand shore of its origin, and takes the boy with it. The water of the sea is, however, unlike that of the lake. It is a force which produces new images, thousands of them. The archetypal foam is full of bubble-dreams, visions of worlds possible if evanescent.

All of this shows us that once the imagination touches matter in reverie, it produces multivalent, excessive beauty, and psychic well-being. Notice, for example, the healthful activity of the little sand crabs who are so obviously seen as aggressively tanned by the sun. Reverie has dislodged and jostled the very adjectives that describe their behavior out of their familiar positions: they are imagined as dynamic and moving, tumbled, salt-wet, scuttling brown. If given free rein, reverie often plays with words in this fashion, creating surprise by new syntactic relationships among words, but there are never any violent eruptions of nonsense which are irreducible to meaning. In the unconscious field we may experience a complete lapsus of the word; in reverie the archetypal element, the substance being imagined, controls the play of linguistic signs. In this world the cold splash of the waves provides a material resistance and meaning stimulating to the imagination, a kind of joyful intentionality that experiences a force in directing itself towards an object. It is altogether different from the sweating adversity of the boy's bed clothes.

In the third and final phase, Johnny returns to the real world which is seen as refreshed, and moving faster from his reverie activity. The ocean breeze has soothed his body—again, an indication of how the unreflective emotive intentions of reverie act magically to transform the world by influencing the body. The summer world is spanked into crisp life, a metaphor of rebirth, of course, but perhaps also recalling the image of the doctor who picked up the shell. There is not as yet a completely independent fantastic world however. It is only the real world which has been rejuvenated. But by virtue of this experience of imaginary meaning sustained by acts of consciousness based on archetypal matter, by the fact that its beautiful and new images are born in the dreamer's solitude away from the real world of perception, by virtue of the fact that the dreamer ventures far away to recover these riches, and by virtue of the well-being it creates, we can call this passage a successful reverie. That the child is a persistent day-dreamer is indicated in a narrator's summary that follows this passage, a passage which estimates the value of the shell in days to come. It is a means to keep temporality flowing onwards toward the future.

There is one aspect of reverie which we first mentioned in our brief summary in the introduction that as yet we have not discussed, namely, its cosmic power of origination. This is actually the most important dimension of reverie, but I have put off discussion of it until the fourth narrative sequence because it is made thematic for the reader there. The fourth sequence is a cognitive attempt at a "philosophy of childhood." The reader is asked to consider the child's desire and imagination in a much larger context which reflects the possibilities of man as a conscious being. There is an allusion from the repertoire to the *Rubaiyat* of Omar Khayyam (whose verse form, the *rubā'ī,* was said to have been accidentally discovered by a poet who overheard the gleeful shout of a child at play and adopted it) to aid the reader in understanding the problem of the conflict or problematic opposition of the world of childhood and the adult's world. The dialogue takes the form of a lesson about the necessity, from the adult's point of view, of acquiring the attributes of maturity: waiting, planning, and above all being patient (there is probably a pun on being a patient and impatience). Yet there is no doubt where the sympathy of the reader should lie, because the mother herself feels the loss of her own childhood in the eyes of her son, which are wide and full of the blue light of his imaginary ocean. Her lesson is therefore somewhat reversed on her.

Now, the boy has learned through the persistence of his daydream the power of cosmic origination in reverie. With that power the boy can say "no" to the adult world even as the new world of reverie opens up for him (symbolically expressed by the shell which he keeps listening to and putting against his ear throughout the lesson). He is no longer completely captive in the world of adults, and we have seen him play with this new-found power (which some parental readers may find anxiety-provoking) in the narrated daydream of the third sequence. Iser might say that what the child has learned, though he cannot at this stage explicitly formulate it, is that his acts are not determined. Imaginative acts of consciousness are caused by nothing but consciousness itself; indeed, they are the characteristic free functioning of childhood consciousness (as readers, we share these acts of imaginative consciousness and spontaneously give our own as well, so it can be said that they are characteristic of adult consciousness as well—a point which I will elaborate in my summary of the reader's discovery in this text). Johnny is a free, if perhaps not entirely responsible, agent. His great discovery is that there is a world of oneiric possibility superadded to the world of reality. The boy is not restricted to the real, for he can enter at will the realm of the ideal through the reverie object. He has the power to negate the actual and actualize the merely possible. Why should he not be intoxicated with this magic power (the sea foam is compared to suds of beer, we remember) and be very reluctant to give it up. Most importantly, however, the child's accession to the freedom of reverie is a break with reality, a rupture which refuses the adult world in creating its own. Johnny's questioning and contrary attitude in this sequence is an important indication that he finds the adult world inadequate and incomplete. The child's imagination is not, therefore, perception revivified, but a characteristic function of human consciousness which transforms the world by the power of negation.

As the end of the third sequence, Johnny had asked his mother about going to the seashore as soon as possible (he imagines the sea as being better than Fox Lake) not being willing to wait for his father's two-week vacation in July. Now the mother tries to teach him patience:

> Mother sat down on the bed and held his hand. The things she said he couldn't understand fully, but some of them made sense. 'If I had to write a philosophy of children, I guess I'd title it impatience. Impatience with everything in life . . . You're a tribe of potential Omar Khayyams, that's what.'' (p. 391)

She reminds him of the attributes of maturity and he responds:

> "I don't wanna be patient. I don't like being in bed. I want to go to the sea shore.'' (p. 391)

The mother tries to mediate the problem of childhood by offering an example from her own childhood:

> "I remember, I saw a doll once when I was a girl. I told my mother about it, said it was the last one for sale, I said I was afraid it would be sold before I could get it. The truth of the matter is there were a dozen others just like it. I couldn't wait. I was impatient, too.''
> Johnny shifted on the bed. His eyes widened and got full of blue light. "But Mom, I don't want to wait. If I wait too long, I'll be grown up, and then it won't be any fun.'' (p. 391)

Obviously, the mother does not want the boy to lie about how well he feels, but the boy's remark about the adult world stifling the fun of things (it doesn't matter how *many* dolls, or sea shells, there are in truth, he seems to say, what matters is having one as a reverie object for one's childhood—otherwise, what would one have to look back on from adulthood if one was never allowed to develop reveries during this precious time) brings the mother to the brink of tears:

"...Sometimes I think you're—right. But I don't dare tell you. It isn't according to the rules—"

"What rules, Mom?"

"Civilization's. Enjoy yourself, while you are young. Enjoy yourself, Johnny." She said it strong, and funny-like.

Johnny put the shell to his ear. "Mom. Know what I'd like to do? I'd like to be at the seashore right now, running towards the water, holding my nose and yelling, 'Last one in is a double-darned monkey!'" Johnny laughed.

The phone rang downstairs. Mother walked to answer it.

Johnny lay there, quietly, listening. (pp. 391-392)

Teaching the reader an unexpected lesson about the necessity of childhood reverie, the mother's attempt to mediate the values of civilization and its discontents (the renunciation of reverie, if not of instinct) to the child has backfired. The equivalences she offers as a bridge of understanding all fail before the boy's desire. She must listen to the pragmatic voices of the adult world, symbolized by the telephone, while her son listens to the call of the sea. Putting the shell to his ear, the child again makes a gesture of commitment to his reverie world. This kind of reversal of intention will be repeated at the end of the last sequence when the mother puts the shell to her ear and hears supernatural voices; in fact she hears the exact same words: "Last one in is a double-darned monkey." This doubling or echoing shatters the framework of everyday reality as her own son becomes a supernatural Other transforming her world from the "outside," that is, from the world within the shell. Thus the reader is made familiar here with a challenging phrase that will return to surprise and perhaps mock him in a fantastic mode. It could be argued that this repetition brings about an uncanny effect of meaning in the reader, but it is actually more in the nature of a fulfillment of meaning postulated as an empty intention earlier.

Certainly it intensifies the problem of a "philosophy of childhood" of whose meaning we might have thought ourselves master. We learn that the language and attitude towards the problem of childhood expressed by the mother, while pretending to be univocal, actually admits to having a double meaning. Children are a potential tribe of Omar Khayyams, always wanting to shatter the schema of things and refashion it closer to the heart's desire (the XCIX stanza of the *Rubaiyat*). Thus the phrase "to have fun with," repeated several times in the story, comes to mean quite different things to the mother than to the boy. The mother thinks that the schema of things, the harsh rule of the reality principle and civilization, cannot be broken, but in the story's marvelous ending, they are. This surprise causes the reader to reexamine the nature of the relationship between imagination and reality, to reconsider a philosophy which represses what childhood reverie does with language, and to formulate for himself the ways in which that schema, which seems so solid, can be broken together with the value of breaking it.

The mother/anima figure raises the possibility that a philosophy of childhood could be written. Bachelard's texts affirm that it can, although in ways subtly subversive of philosophic conceptual mastery itself. We ourselves have been reading (or rather writing about) this story as if it were an allegory of childhood and reverie, as if the entire text had the effect of being an illustration of that idea. As Todorov points out, this procedure is a meta-reading which to an extent falsifies the all-important temporal and experiential structure of fantasy texts. Knowing the end destroys the function of hesitation on which the genre seems to depend.[7] For Todorov, the fantastic is a genre of "emphatic temporality." It is essential in his view that a reading of the fantastic follow that of the reader in his identification with a character step by irreversible step. We too want to follow the flow of reading and not to impose artificial constructs, yet this procedure is justified here because the reader's double role in "The Sea Shell" directs him to reconsider retrospectively and reflectively the relationship of imagination to reality he held prior to reading. In philosophical terms, when the empty schema of the shell is marvelously "filled in" with supernatural voices at the end, we wonder how the boy manages to be absent from the world yet present in language at the same time. Our allegorical reading does not therefore destroy the effect of the fantastic, so much as it does thematize how that effect is brought about through the experience of the imaginary, the ontological significance of which the reader has to search for at the end. Let us therefore consider how the themes and elements of the fantastic emerge in the fifth sequence.

There is first of all the reader's hesitation (constituting what in Todorov's view is the evanescent theoretical genre of the pure fantastic) about the supernatural voices that emerge from the shell. Is the boy imagining them or are they real? The narrator gives us no indication but records the character's own surprise and hesitation on hearing them. We are still very much in the adult scheme of things at the beginning of this sequence. However, a dynamic tension between two landscapes is again conveyed through an oneiric window-metaphor: stars are caught in the squared glass corrals of the big window. This suggested equivalence brings about a child's view of the night sky's constellations as brightly moving animal figures that have been imprisoned, and lends a sense of cosmic sympathy to the boy's situation. But from this confining boundary or frame to the end of the story, the events move away from the world of everyday reality to end in what Todorov would classify as a fantastic-marvelous situation, defined as a hesitation between the real and the imaginary where the supernatural has not yet been accepted.[8] Following the character's emotive intentions, the reader has thus far assumed that Johnny was imagining that shore inside the shell, but now autonomous voices appear:

> Johnny closed his eyes. Downstairs, silverware was being clattered at the dinner table. Mom and Pop were eating. He heard Pop laughing his deep laughter.

The waves still came in, over and over, on the shore inside the sea shell. And—something else.

"Down where the waves lift, down where the waves play, down where the gulls swoop low on a summer's day—"

"Huh? Johnny listened. His body stiffened. He blinked his eyes.

Softly, way off:

"Stark ocean sky, sunlight on waves. Yo ho, heave ho, heave ho, my braves—"

It sounded like a hundred voices singing to the creak of oar-locks.

"Come down to the sea in ships—"

And then another voice, all by itself, soft against the sound of waves and ocean wind. "Come down to the sea, the contortionist sea, where the great tides wrestle and swell. Come down to the salt in the glittering brine, on a trail that you'll soon know well—"

Johnny pulled the shell from his head, stared at it.

"Do you want to come down to the sea, my lad, do you want to come down to the sea? Well, take me by the hand, my lad, just take me by the hand, my lad, and come along with me!"

Trembling, Johnny clamped the shell to his ear again, sat up in bed, breathing fast. His small heart leaped and hit the wall of his chest. (p. 392)

The presence of these legendary voices is full of the dynamic activity the child desires. They could be pirates or Sinbad the sailor's men, a tribe of potential Omar Khayyams. Interacting with the sea by rowing rhythmically, they chant of magical pathways among the waves. But we do not respond merely to linguistic speech acts. There is again the attraction of shining, gleaming, glittering things from a landscape brilliant but unseen. Bright colors, pungent smells, and seductive words and gestures call for the boy to immerse himself in their collective action. Then a single voice separates itself from this chanting and invites him to come down to the "contortionist" sea "on a path that you'll soon know well." The very idea of the sea as a contortionist suggests the acrobatic transformation of the self into some extraordinary fantastic position. The ordinary and regular paths of the adult world (which the boy has spent so much time emotively negating) are to be magically replaced by a trail the boy will soon know well by some slight of hand. Clearly, the voice anticipates his inmost desire, surprising and shattering his expectations. The voice comes from the realm of the supernatural Other, but it is nevertheless a guiding voice that tells him he will soon be very familiar with something. It thus quickly establishes its benign nature by mimicking the anima's safe and gradual guidance. It may be demonic, but the surrounding voices are soft, insistent, and Johnny's small heart leaps at the thought of taking part in such rhythmic activity, and by this we know he is already magically transforming his body to meet it. The dialectics of inside and out takes one more step in telling Johnny that the path to the sea-water world lies in the mysterious imagination of the shell's exterior form (the mother had directed his attention to the inside after luring him with exterior prettiness):

"Have you ever seen a fine conch-shell, shaped and shined like a pearl corkscrew? It starts out big and it ends up small, seemingly ending with nothing at all, but, aye lad, it ends where the sea-cliffs fall; where the sea-cliffs fall to the blue!" (p. 392)

These internally rhyming lines contain the pleasure of novelty and surprise (in seeing words dissimilar in meaning appear similar in sound) while creating a kind of enclosing spell. The spiral is a syntheseis of both big and small, a path of infinite imagination that only seems to end up with nothing (complete negation and loss of the real) but actually reveals its own world in the frozen image of a wave at play. Johnny recognizes that the shell points in an imaginary direction, out of this world:

> Johnny's fingers tightened on the circular marks of the shell. That was right. It went around and around and around until you couldn't see it going around any more.
> Johnny's lips tightened. What was it mother had said? Children. The—the philosophy—what a big word! of children! Impatience. Impatience! Yes, yes, he was impatient! Why not? His free hand clenched into a tiny hard white fist, pounding against the covers. (p. 393)

The last gesture is indeed a magical action! Johnny's hand has become a wave pounding on the beach. He has transformed his mother's philosophy of children into action, by making his hand into the image of a wave. Why not, he thinks, negating the adult world, and the reader may find that he himself has accepted these supernatural events as marvelous, as Johnny seems to here. At any rate, we can understand why he chooses to hide the precious shell from his father when he comes to say goodnight. The world of the child should remain separate from the adult world, we feel.[9] Yet the reader's fear-curiosity complex *is* aroused. In the mother's philosophy, the shell can always be removed from one's ear, one's impatience having been temporarily assuaged, and it is therefore an object belonging to the larger instrumental complex of the adult world. But if the shell is itself a world, then the boy is lost to us. As I have mentioned, some readers may feel a strong sense of menace in the way these voices seem to anticipate his reactions. However, I find the subliminal suggestion of fear so softened by the boy's obvious enjoyment and well-being in the reverie world that I do not fear for him at all. My fear and surprise are rather for the mother in the last sequence.

The sixth and final sequence is told from the mother's point of view, that is, from the point of view of one who possesses the philosophic attributes of maturity, but also an embarrassed sympathy for the child's imagination. At the end of the fifth sequence, we are held in suspense, wondering whether the voices will be seen to be illusory or not. We carry forward our hesitation into this last sequence, which at first seems to modulate towards what Todorov calls the supernatural explained (the uncanny). But the story then spirals down to a surprise ending—a quality which is difficult to capture in quotation. First of all the boy *is* absent from the scene, we do not as yet know where, but all the familiar objects the boy has invested with emotive intentions return. Through a succession of empty objects that are nevertheless subliminally suggested as filled (and this juxtaposition leads the reader, but not the mother, to the oneiric level) we can feel that the boy has escaped:

> The bed was empty. There was nothing but sunlight and silence in the room. Sunlight lay abed, like a bright patient with its brilliant head on the pillow. The quilt, a red-blue circus banner, was thrown back. The bed was wrinkled like the face of a pale old man, and it was very empty. (p. 393)

Daydreaming sunlight, which emanates from the outside world, has taken Johnny's place. The circus banner that confined him is thrown back, abandoned, which reveals the bed itself as transformed to an old man, wrinkled and empty. These images go beyond the obvious rejection-of-adulthood motif—they hint at a transformation of self to a world where youth is forever preserved against the onset of adulthood. They suggest a world transcended. The mother hypothesizes that the child has run outside to play with "those neighbor ruffians." As the mother begins to adjust the quilt into place (trying to rearrange things back to the paths of the ordinary and orderly world) and to smooth the sheets, she discovers that the bed is *not* empty. The shell is there. It appears again as unfamiliar in perception. The mother brings forth "a shining object into the sun." This image hints again at the rebirth motif, for a child is unfamiliar to its mother at birth. She smiles, recognizing it as familiar, and perhaps to remember her own childhood or her son who she assumes is now absent, puts the shell to her ear "just for fun" and receives the shock of her life:

> The room whirled around in a bright swaying merry-go-round of bannered quilts and glassed run.
> The sea shell roared in her ear. (p. 394)

The mother's sudden vertiginous loss of reality, the shattering of the adult scheme of things, is conveyed by the rapid motion of the merry-go-round, an object which itself bears connotations of the return of childhood time. We feel that she is instantaneously thrown into this fantastic world, which the narrator now presents without comment, leaving an ellipsis or indeterminacy for the reader at the end:

> Waves thundered on a distant shore. Waves foamed cool on a far off beach. (p. 394)

So far, these images are very much like those Johnny discovered in his reverie of the shell, and they could be her reverie, but:

> Then the sound of small feet crunching swiftly in the sand. A high young voice yelling: "Hi! Come on, you guys! Last one in is a double-darned monkey!"
> And the sound of a small body diving, splashing, into those waves . . . (p. 394)

So the story ends, on a fantastic-marvelous event. As Tolkien would perhaps say, the sea shell was no more us than we were it. The reader's spontaneity has been released; the child has become totally Other, transforming the mother's world from the outside (which is also, of course, the inside of a shell). A reverie object of the inside familiar world suddenly reveals its potential to shatter the scheme of things, teaching the mother a lesson in the "philosophy of childhood." The sea shell was an instrument of deferral in the hands of the mother, a world of reverie to the boy, and a means of marvelous escape to whatever supernatural beings seemed to inhabit it. The reader is left with the impossibility of accepting this event as a hallucination—we are given too much of a grounding in the familiar world of the mother to believe that *she* is sick or feverish. Neither can we acquiesce in the pure marvelous, as in a fairy tale, where events of this nature would provoke no surprise. It seems to me that the reader is left with a problem of working out for himself the relationships of imagination and reality that have played back and forth throughout this story.

Summarizing the reader's double role, we can say that the sea shell of our story receives different imaginative values from two perspectives: that of the adult and that of the child. As the story progresses, it functions as a center for intentional acts of consciousness that are instrumental in building up Johnny's sublimative reverie world and in destroying the limited perspectives of the adult world. With the surprise ending the reader is directed towards the oneiric level of the text from which he must build up an adequate "philosophy of childhood." Offering a transcendent vantage point, this level allows the reader to explore existentially his own capacity for reverie. Just as in the experience of the fantastic according to Todorov, the implied reader of "The Sea Shell" is required to judge certain events while identifying himself with a character. Yet these events are so structured by the text that recollecting and anticipatory acts of consciousness on the part of the reader lend it a kind of reflective depth that Bachelard calls reverberation. The reader must built up a system of equivalences between the two perspectives that culminates in the emergence of the aesthetic object, the shell as world. Our surprise at this world "fills in" the passive and provisional syntheses that went before with a more active significance.

Because the shell is only a schema in a story (picking up our allegorical reading again), it solicits us to imagine it, *as* imagined by the characters of the story who represent the norms of the adult and childhood worlds in conflict. The sea shell reverberates with this conflict as it comes to consciousness in the reader's mind. We reexperience their intentions, but the shell itself remains a beautiful formal object. Only its significance changes, due to the affective intentions, strong or weak, of the characters. As long as we remain on the emotive level (which is basically unreflective) we live this story by our own imaginative acts of consciousness. But reverie becomes a magical world *for us*, we double ourselves in the midst of the pragmatic world we have for the moment suspended. The story would not be able to have the effect on us that it does (the search for the meaning of childhood imagination) if we did not constitute it, however unreflectively, for ourselves first. In that regard, we can agree with Todorov. But the last magical transformation of the shell defeats our expectations, surprises us. We are confronted with our own emotive acts of consciousness as magical,—the very ones we used to constitute a fantastic world—and as we see the mother's world transformed into a dizzying merry-go-round by the supernatural Other. We realize that the shell has been made to conform to the child's ideal image of it, that is, as a world of oneiric activity apart from the adult world, containing him—what he wanted it to be all along. The boy's feelings, we realize, have remade the world closer to his heart's desire. How this occurrence came about we are not told, the text remains in the fantastic-marvelous, and we must re-search the problematic relation between the real and the imaginary.

The reader's unreflective imaginary possession of this story and its reverie object, the sea shell, will lead him later to several discoveries about reverie itself, which we are now prepared to summarize. First of all, we can say that "The Sea Shell" has enriched our understanding of the relationship between the imagination of childhood and the largely perceptual (or so Bradbury presents it) world of adults. Perceptual objects, like the shell, yield themselves only by degrees, never all at once, as in the magical image. There is great pleasure in considering objects for their formal beauty, but their real value can be discovered only by inhabiting them. Second, we realize that should the sea shell have appeared unaccompanied by imaginative transformation, we would have experienced a singularly impoverished world. The childhood imagination in reverie seeks to change the merely perceived by making up for what is lacking in the adult world. Lastly, this magical and emotive transformation of things closer to the heart's desire *is* based on what is known in perception, but it is not merely a reproduction of it. In reverie the image-making powers of the mind are a synthesis of the emotive and the cognitive.

Considered as an objective verbal document, "The Sea Shell" is not the equal in style to some of Bradbury's later accomplishments with object reveries in the context of the family, which we will examine in later chapters. It has a tendency to make its theme—a philosophy of childhood—all too sentimentally obvious. Nevertheless, Bradbury does use those phenomenological elements of the reading process we have outlined—recognition and grounding in the familiar repertoire, expectation, imagistic surprise which then leads to discovery—to enable the reader to constitute one of the major themes of all his work, namely, a philosophy of childhood. The reader of "The Sea Shell' discovers a resultant world composed on the basis of the old and familiar adult world, but yet entirely new and unique, transformed by childhood imagination. As in all texts based on reverie, the reader is compelled to imagine an intimate relation with the cosmos and to wonder at the sudden illumination of the image which opens on another fantastic world.

A sophisticated reader might be inclined to smile at such childish enthusiasms. But Bradbury, in having the reader identify with his character, Johnny Bishop, really returns him to the thing itself, the sea shell, as constituted by a purely phenomenological consciousness, which, because of its extreme naiveté, is without preconceptions. We follow the naive consciousness of the boy imagining the sea shell and gather for ourselves images that suggest a sublimatory capacity for renewal. The reader discovers, in short, a rebirth of his own childhood imagination. Inside the small shell time speeds up in marvelous ways, distance is magically abolished, the reader's imagination bathes in the cosmic rhythms of the sea. Bradbury's formal re-imagining of the shell's spiral has generated a story which begins with traditional images and associations but which does not allow the reader to crawl slowly into the shell and subsist in repose. Johnny has left the sea shell behind, in the hands of the anima figure who gave it to him, for fun. He has transcended the parental "Omar Khayyam complex." He has gone on to dream in his element, water, and the reader may well surmise that the real hero of the story is the doctor, who must have known that a child who cannot imagine surely suffers a worse fate than one who can, no matter how ill, when he picked up the sea shell along the sounding shore.

Reverie and the Gothic

"Cistern" (1947) is a sombre and melancholy story about a middle-aged woman's suicide by drowning in the cisterns beneath a rain-filled city. That event is the single narrative action of the story, but it is nevertheless a death prepared by a long reverie in which the desired element of death is water. Anna, the gray old maid of the story, wants to accede to a guiltless and beautiful state of being in which she and her lost lover, Frank, can enjoy a kind of innocent childlike sexuality. In her reverie, they are transformed into Japanese paper flowers that open and blossom in the presence of rain water; otherwise they lead a dry, artificial existence in their arcanum beneath the city. In this limbo of less-than-being, there would be no blame attached to their acts because they would be dead, or so she fantasizes, and they could only be resurrected in some rainy season of the imagination. The reader soon learns that Anna's melancholy is the result of fear and repression and disgust at the sexual act. However, our cognitive discovery in this story is in part to discern what happens to the imagination when it is repressed—it threatens to become uncanny or wholly other. Anna's sister, Juliet, represents the fear of fantasy in the story and it is her perspective that we are finally led to reject.

Death and catacombs have of course become clichés in the literature of the Gothic, but because the presence of reverie is so strong in the story they do not evoke horror. Rather, the mood is closer to romantic melancholy.[1] In Anna's reverie this very melancholy and mourning is transformed into a world that gives natural continuity to her existence. Her reverie moves towards an aesthetic and sensuous fulfillment involving her whole being. Anna uses images as actions in narrating her reverie to Juliet and therefore her frigidity is sublimated by reverie into a cold water that stimulates her. Anna wants, however, and unlike Johnny Bishop our other dreamer of water, to be completely determined (ravished) by the element she imagines. Only it will be responsible for amorous advances. As paper flower, she cannot be blamed for any responses she may have in return. The cistern, like the sea shell, provides an oneiric space of refuge for her reverie, but as it progresses, we sense the appeal of water for a consciousness which wants a passive, floating state of being.

In short, a different complex is organizing the production of surface imagery in this story, although both are involved with water and dreams. In terms of oneiric criticism, we can discern the emergence of the Ophelia complex and the transformation of its dynamic image: a woman's hair unloosened by the water. Shakespeare's Ophelia is part of the repertoire of this text, and the motif of the floating-haired drowned woman will be familiar to most readers. According to Bachelard, activation of the Ophelia complex allows images of young and beautiful flowered death *(la mort fleurie)* to appear in consciousness.[2] This complex unites a mixture of grace, madness, and despair with a fascination for water which masks a desire to destroy oneself. And if, Bachelard asserts, a writer renews the dynamic image of this complex (the floating hair) by pushing its idealization further, then he makes use of the complex under its "good form."[3] Under its bad form, the culture complex remains a painful blockage to the unfolding of consciousness. Potentially, however, and under its "good" form, the culture complex is a transformer of psychic energy. Because it is grafted upon deeper fantasy levels of the collective unconscious, a dreamer who awakens the effort of cultural sublimation present in the complex will also awaken the desire for transcendence, to sublimate its images further, to make them more beautiful; hence the production of the oneiric level of significance according to Bachelard.

In order to discuss the action of this complex in terms of literary style, Bachelard isolated a dynamic image or node from it, one that would have the "role of creative detail" in reveries based on it—as we have already mentioned, the image of floating hair unloosened by the water is the most suggestive aspect of the Ophelia complex. When Bachelard allowed himself to reverberate to this vision of the floating hair, he discovered that "it by itself animates an entire symbol of the psychology of waters, that it explains almost by itself the entire Ophelia complex."[4] Nevertheless if Ophelia becomes her hair, she is more than a rhetorical figure. Bachelard is careful to emphasize that details of style reveal a basic mode of existence in a fantastic world.

It is these details or nuances of meaning that Bachelard records as he studies the action of the Ophelia complex from myth to folktale to modern narratives. Sometimes the appearance of weeds floating in a stream is enough to activate the complex. Sometimes in the rocks of a ford where a woman has drowned, poets imagine that they can see the stream play like living hair; sometimes a unsuspecting man comes too close to a mysterious (and probably supernatural) woman combing her hair on a bridge. Suddenly, the man is seized by the hair and thrown into the river to drown. We already know how deeply Poe's oneiric temperament was marked by heavy melancholy water *(l'eau lourde),* so we are not surprised to learn that this dynamic image of unloosened, fallen hair awakens in Poe the desire to drown "in a bath of the tresses of Annie." These are just a few examples culled from a chapter that includes discussion of Shakespeare, the source of the image, Mallarme, Balzac, Rimbaud, Rilke, Claudel and many others. Of course we can assume that none of these writers have ever actually *seen* a drowned young woman; it is a question of imagined images in a literary tradition of the fantastic.

To be sure, few of Bradbury's stories arc as carefully plotted for effect as Poe's grotesque and arabesques. He is often dismissed as an epigone of Poe by critics.[5] Nevertheless in "Cistern" Bradbury is dealing with what Poe claimed as the very core of his aesthetic: the notion that the death of a beautiful woman is the most appropriate theme for poetic inspiration. And dealing with it in such a way that it gives rise not to the repetition compulsion of the unconscious fantasy, but to reverie as existential possibility.

As opposed to what we may know about the reasons for suicide in the real world, literacy suicides by their very nature as fictional constructs can never lack aesthetic means and ends to stimulate the reader's fantasy. They are, after all, at the disposal of the implied author. Even when he may wish to hide them, or to leave the matter blank as an indeterminacy, the reader will still search for them, perhaps the more because they are hidden. Therefore, argues Bachelard, the determinism of literacy suicide is everywhere on display. Murder and literary crime may not be at all in keeping with character and may erupt from external circumstances with considerable verisimilitude. Murder mystery deals with the reader's search for a realm of objective facts; by contrast, literary suicide must pose its problems more intimately than this if it is to be successful in calling forth a response.[6] Bradbury uses this literary determinism of suicide against itself by displaying intimately the interior world of his main character, Anna, and by showing us a fantastic world in which she realizes her desires. But Anna's long reverie of inhabiting the cistern creates a subliminal suspense and understanding that is only released at the end when she decides to actually commit suicide. We only hear the cistern lid rising and slamming down, as Juliet does, but unlike her we cannot hope that Anna will return. The reader discovers that Anna's choice of death is a necessary fulfillment of the meaning of her tortured existence, and may in fact be a transcendence of it. In particular there is a playful and dreaming inversion of the Ophelia complex in "Cistern" which makes it into a transformer of psychic energy for Anna and for the reader who delights in the cosmic cycle of her journey. Disgust and shame are kept at bay by this oneiric level of significance. By becoming passive in reverie, Anna paradoxically becomes more active than she had ever hoped to be in real life. She identifies her body with her hair and becomes one with the current of the water which carries her around the world with her lover. Indeed there is so much unrepressed life in her reverie that it is difficult to view her death as anything but a free choice.

On the oneiric level of significance, "Cistern" also transforms one of the major themes of the fantastic dealing with sexuality and desire: the double. According to Todorov, the themes of the other (to which the double belongs) are frequently formed out of the relationship established between two interlocutors during their discourse. Fantastic events may not be directly observed but instead may be spoken in the presence of another character.[7] This distinction will enable us to affirm that "Cistern" is a fantastic text because of its rhetorical discourse. Anna recounts a reverie world of supernatural ideal love in which she and her dead lover are united. However, many of the stronger emotions usually evoked by the Gothic, including disgust at the corruption of the dead being juxtaposed right alongside the living, and the fantasy of necrophilia in which the body of the dead lover is voluptuously caressed, are sublimated by an *anima-animus dialectic*. I have indicated before that the nature of Bachelardian reverie is essentially and deeply feminine, and that the anima is the principle of continuous, tranquil being. In Bachelard's poetics of reverie (which is of course a poetics of reading) the anima dreams and sings, but the animus, the male principle of the psyche, is concerned to narrate the facts of a situation objectively, is involved with projects and worries, with ways of not being present to itself. This is of course very different from Todorov's poetics, which emphasizes Freudian fantasy and the uncanny aspects of the other.

In reverie, the anima and animus are brought into balance by a series of criss-crossing projections. A kind of intimate dialectics develops according to Bachelard when we are led by reverie to idealize our feminine and masculine unconscious images, which do not belong to the social realm, but to the archetypes of the collective unconscious. The result is that we no longer consider the social rivalry of the sexes. The masculine and feminine principles of our being communicate in tranquility their desire for a well-harmonized double nature and idealize their passion. The anima which dreams and the animus which observes are brought into a balance which Bachelard calls dreaming observation *(l'obser-vation rêveuse)*.[8] Bachelard represents the schema of idealization involving two psyches as a quadrangle with anima and animus at opposite poles, but since this can only appeal to mechanically minded readers I choose not to reproduce it here. Besides, since our character is a woman, we will only be concerned with the idealizing forces of the feminine.

In our story, Anna projects the masculine ideal, a figure who embodies those masculine values she desires to come to her from the outside. Furthermore, she doubles herself again by imagining her own anima as the projected ideal of her lover. In this manner Anna as dreamer is led by the anima to examine all the idealizations of being loved, and to dream the communion of masculine and feminine, the two principles of integral being. Anna's reverie allows her to explore regions of doubling that are supernatural, but not threatened by the phantasmagorical beings of the fantastic. On the contrary, Anna dreams of a being who would cure her solitude, even though he be dead. Anna's reverie makes her a double in another world, yet she remains at home with herself; the man and woman of her reverie are contained in one person, even when magnified and split so that her lover, Frank, can also be doubled into anima and animus. It goes without saying that reverie splits our being more naturally, more gently than that which Todorov ascribes to the poetics of the fantastic. Nevertheless, there are intensities of being which accompany this process and which give rise to a number of ontological paradoxes:

> Isn't this the first of the ontological paradoxes: by transporting the dreamer into another world, reverie makes the dreamer into a person different from himself. And yet this person is still himself, the double of himself. Literature on "the double" is not lacking. . . But these "splittings" are extreme cases where, in some way, the bonds between the two split personalities are broken. Reverie — and not the dream — retains mastery over its splittings. . . . And thus it is that the being projected by reverie — for our I-dreamer is a projected being — is double as we ourselves are, and is, like ourselves, *animus* and *anima*. Here we are at the knot of all our paradoxes: the *"double" is the double of a double being.*
>
> Then, in the most solitary reveries, when we call forth vanished beings, when we idealize the persons who are dear to us, when in our readings we are free enough to live as man and woman, we feel that all of life takes on a double — that the past takes on a double, that all beings become double in their idealization, that the world incorporates all the beauties of our chimeras.[9]

By splitting the personality in such extreme ways, the literature of the fantastic based on the nocturnal dream, Bachelard goes on to argue, never allows us to make it truly ours. I might add that even in Jungian analysis the experience of the anima can be seductively dangerous (the witch is one of the primary manifestations of the anima according to Jung), but never in Bachelardian reverie. But that as it may, we are now in a position to present our analysis of "Cistern" and to discern whether it evinces the harmonious double character of idealized love to which Bachelard refers, and whether her reverie world incorporates that beauty. We will see whether Anna is mistress of all her splittings.

To begin with, Anna's reverie flows through a cistern that is hidden from the eyes of the living inhabitants of the city. The network of catacomb-like cisterns underlies and doubles the streets of the city. It is not presented as a fearsome labyrinth, however, but rather as an echoing space for her reverie which when filled with water enables her to travel all through it with playful ease. And the inhabitants of these catacombs are not really dead. "Being dead" represents the penumbral being of childhood before the loss of the love object (perhaps the Freudian latency period). Ontologically, it is a warm and exciting region of play that has not yet confronted non-being or lack. More precisely and in Anna's own terms, to inhabit a cistern is to enjoy a fantasy of invisibility because one has not yet *come out:* "It's a nice goose-pimply, rainy-day feeling like when you were a child and played hide-and-seek and nobody found you and there you were in their midst all the time . . ." (p. 269).[10]

On the level of material imagination and reverie, Anna's dream-landscape is also doubled into two climates, the season of the shadowy and wet and the season of the dry when the cistern is full of heat and sunshine. Considered as a totality, however, it is a single archetypal image of the natural cycle dominated by rain. Anna's reverie flows through a succession of happy, sometimes erotic and even whimsical images. The germinating image of her reverie is given in the following lines by the narrator, as Anna is sitting at the window seat, looking out on the world from within a protected space (a situation already emblematic of the developing subjectivity of reverie): "The rain scrambled in wild pushing pellets down the window. Drops came and joined with others and made streaks." (p. 270).

Now the appeal of this image is first to the dynamic imagination and second to the underlying element. The wild pushing pellets suggest to the imagination the stirring movement of erotic sensation through the skin, the joining of the raindrops the meeting of two lovers. Anna's reverie will take its oneiric impetus from the flowing of water. Its narrative shape and style are governed by water; her eyelids raise and lower themselves in "gentle pulsations, as if she were about to tell a long story and knew it and wanted to work into it slowly, and then faster and faster, until the very momentum of the story would carry her on . . ." (p. 271). Anna will first tell of the animus, Frank, and how he came to be in the cistern (though of course she does not use his real name), and then of the anima, her double, who has recently joined him, as the disapproving dialogue with Juliet pulls out more and more layers of significance belonging to her dream which the narrator tells us is also a decision of some kind. We only come to understand her dream as a choice when the story ends. That decision is contained potentially in the world of the first image, and it is evident that the experience of reverie has in fact already taken place when Anna begins to narrate:

> Anna whispered. "All this water put me to sleep awhile, I guess, and then I began to think about the rain and where it came from and where it went and how it went down those little slots in the curb and then I thought about deep under and suddenly there *they* were." (p. 270)

When Anna drifts "deep under' towards the unconscious, she finds her being surprisingly doubled in the image of two supernatural lovers brought together by the rain. But she experiences no anguish at this doubling; in fact, Anna's first contact with her desired element allows her to become mistress of all her doublings, as is evident from the way in which she handles the disparaging remarks of her sister Juliet that follow immediately on the passage quoted above. In each response and question, Juliet reveals a cruder and more fearful imagination than her sister. At times, she seems to take Anna's statements absolutely literally in trying to point out their absurdity. How could two people be living together for years in the cistern, she asks indignantly? It is actually she who imagines two people crawling down there to make carnal love when what Anna has in mind is obviously some kind of spiritual transformation. Juliet thinks such people must be insane to want to live together in such a place; Anna reveals that subtle ontological paradox that the man and woman are *dead*.

If we place the initial image of Anna's reverie in another oneiric moment later in the text, we can capture its growing reverberation more dramatically. Here Anna describes laughingly to Juliet (who now wants her to stop talking about it entirely) "how its starts," that is, how the man and woman exist during the wet season. She says: "At first all the upper world is pellets. Street cars run by all pimply" (p. 272). We are again made aware that the place of reverie is the body. But when these pellets gather together, a bit further on in her reverie, we find an archetype of the collective unconscious emerging:

"It seeps down. Then, in all the other hollows come other seepages. Little twines and snakes. Tobacco-stained water. It makes puddles. Then it—moves. It joins others. It makes snakes and then one big constrictor which rolls along on the flat-papered floor, with a majestic movement. From everywhere, from north and south, from other streets, other streams come and they make one hissing and shining of coils." (p. 273)

The final fulguration of this sequence, the shining coils of a gigantic snake, is quite sufficient to make us feel the oneiric impetus of its sexual theme. Sensation, according to Bachelard, can be experienced oneirically as a serpent: "Yes, sensation flees, hot one moment in gushing energy, then cold, it slides, it does not have a pattern, it undulates in the muscles, under the skin, swelling the thighs like a large reptile."[11] Anna has aroused the primitive and powerful force of the serpent's coils, yet by further imagining it in its archetypal activity, she will sublimate it. For Anna's dynamic imagination, the serpent is an interlacing, tactile being: it loves to entwine upon itself. It suggests to Anna an oneiric logic of invention in which she may become her own reverie object by doubling on herself.

Throughout her reverie, Anna uses her hands expressively to represent the man and woman of her "little dream." This kind of hand puppetry indicates that both figures are present in one body:

"They touch their hands and lips and when they come into a cross-street outlet of the cistern the tide rushes them together and they burn cold in the water!" She clapped her hands together. (p. 275)

The burning coldness of the sensation here suggests something of the continued ambivalence of the sexual for Anna, and reveals to the reader the frigidity of her ontological condition which subsumes mere problems of sexual maladjustment. Anna aspires to be neither dead not alive, neither cold not hot, but to live in some unressurrected ontological state that is prior to these oppositions yet which contains them both.

The role of the serpent in this transformation is a familiar one to archetypal critics. The snake-like phallus-demon appears beside the Great Mother as a residuum of the originally androgynous nature of the unconscious in many myths.[12] But since it is a question here of active fantasy, the numinous powers of the masculine are not allowed to become too demonic. They are gradually assimilated to Anna's desires. Our dreamer valorizes only certain aspects of this archetype: its nakedness (due to its shedding of skin): "A man and a woman, with no clothing on, in the water. . ." (p. 275), its mobility, the way it can disappear quickly into the slots of the cistern and hide, and finally its ability to be master of the earth: "They can go anywhere they want, all over the earth, on a deep siphon, and come back later. . ." (p. 276). This latter aspect indicates that Anna joins all prodigious dreamers in pushing her dream to the cosmic level.

But the serpent's real power over Anna's imagination is the deep seduction of its coils, the node of energy of this archetype which appears at the end of the passage quoted above. It is the masculine strength of this seduction by matter which she draws on in reverie to overcome her strongly ambivalent attitude towards Frank and sexuality: "But if I had held onto him he'd have been revolted and so would I, and Frank would have been shocked and frightened and run off like a little boy, and I'd have hated him if he had touched me" (p. 277). In order to possess and be possessed by her lover, Anna doubles herself, and then sublimates that coiling aggressive energy through the idealization of the Ophelia complex (masculine snake becomes feminine and flower-strewn hair) whose action we can see in the following passage:

> She clasped her hands, slowly, working finger into finger, interlacing.
> "The water soaks into them. First, it lifts the woman's hand. In a little move. Her hand's the only live part of her. Then her arm lifts and one foot. And her hair—" She touched her own hair as it hung about her shoulders. "—unloosens and opens out like a flower in the water. Her shut eyelids are blue . . ."
> The room got darker, Juliet sewed on, and Anna talked and told all she saw in her mind. She told how the water rose and took the woman with it, unfolding her out and loosening her and standing her full upright in the cistern, the dead woman not caring. "The water is interested in the woman, and she lets it have its way. All morals come from outside *to* her. After a long time of lying still, and being stiff, she's ready to live again, any life the water wants her to have." (p. 273)

In this passage we can discern the movement of sublimation, which transforms Anna's whole body into aesthetic sensuousness. The serpent's motion is transferred to Anna's magical and emotive hands as soon as the water, moving upward (symbolically the direction of sublimation), reaches the dry niches where the two "dead" people are lying. In joining her hands, through imaginative acts of consciousness directed at her body, Anna becomes both subject and object of her reverie. Interiorization begins with the soaking in of the water into the papery existence of the Japanese water flowers. Anna imagines the water touching the hands of the woman first, but we should grasp the fact that the water is already the projected masculine ideal. Then gradually the hair unloosens and opens out like a flower in the water, sublimating the image further by laying her head of hair out flat upon the surface of the water where Anna can experience herself as passive.

Anna's dull grey-brown hair is beautified, as are her eyelids, made blue by the matter she imagines.

As previously indicated, the movement of unloosened hair upon the water is the center or node of energy of the Ophelia complex. It is from here that poetic transformations take place. Anna touches her own hair as it hangs about her shoulders, thus activating the passive nature of the hair in being touched. The narrator reports that Anna has *become* her hair. He makes of her hair a synecdoche for her entire body and the passive existence she so actively desires: "unfolding *her* out and unloosening *her*" (my italics). This oneiric logic of invention will allow her to travel all over the world with her lover.

But Anna does not want to intend these actions too overtly; she remains untouched by the punishing remorse of conscience because all morals must come to her from the outside to be distantly allowed or disallowed. Her acts of consciousness are therefore reflexive, she acts upon herself, but not as yet reflective. Any moral consciousness, which could bear an active intentionality coming from the Other, is at the outset bracketed by Anna. In the protected space of the cistern, the Other cannot transform her world with any damning look, and she is not responsible for her actions anyway because she is a passive paper flower which lives the life the water wants it to. In Sartre's terms, all this would represent a pattern of bad faith, yet we should bear in mind that Anna faces up to her anguish at the end by choosing death.

In effect, Anna in her narrative "quotes" the Ophelia complex as a suggested solution to her problem. She then develops it imaginatively as a reader of her own text. She experiences her body as a paper flower soaking in water. Yet by a strange and unfolding ontological paradox, once Anna interiorizes the water and the experience of the imaginary, a sort of determinism in reverse takes place. To be completely determined by the matter one imagines is to be transcendentally free. Sensation and experience then depend on the power of imagination. When she herself considers this aspect of reverie (the paradox that they are dead yet because doubled so alive), the narrator tells us that Anna is quite pleased with herself: "it was a nice discovery and she was proud of it" (p. 270). Throughout her reverie, Anna brings more and more of these pre-reflective discoveries to light, until finally she has to confront herself reflectively. But whenever she thinks of possible critisism of her reverie, she remembers that they would have to be "resurrected" in order to be criticized: "And nobody could do that, it's too late. That's the beauty of it!" (p. 275).

Reverie rejects such an apocalypse. Furthermore, on the oneiric level of the text, the reader is shown Anna's freedom in responding to the unconscious coils of the uroboros, the snake-archetype. Anna actively explores the snake's interest in her and therefore she becomes capable of a wider consciousness. Unconscious processes provide her with a certain context — a complex limiting her response to the world — but she recognizes and develops them, sublimates and masters them creatively, making them much more than just a repressed and mechanical mirror-doubling of her ambivalence:

> She admitted the image she had in her mind. "It takes death to make a woman really beautiful, and it takes death by drowning to make her most beautiful of all. Then all the stiffness is taken out of her and her hair hangs upon the water like a drift of smoke. And her arms and legs and fingers move in the water with such slow purposelessness and she's very water-elegant and water-graceful." (p. 271)

It is the Ophelia complex which gives expression to Anna's desire to die in water, but notice how quickly we slide from beautiful to most beautiful! Unlike Poe's idealized feminine death, this "Annie" manifests a whimsical nature. This is the playful sublimation of a dreamer who does not fear death because there is nothing in it which is foreign to her. She is at home; she has become one with her element, as is indicated by the words she compounds to indicate her fantastic transformation: water-elegant and water-graceful. She outwits all those who might direct, repress, or make judgements about her reverie, including the strictures of her own moral agency, by *playing* dead. Of the anima she says: "She turns every once in awhile to read passing newspapers with unseeing eyes" (p. 271). The anima in reading does not acknowledge anxiety or the enormity of becoming, her blue eyelids shut to events that have long since passed.

Why then does Anna finally choose to die in reality? The only answer to this must lie in her inability to resolve the intolerable ambivalence of her life. The strongest image of this story, the Gothic cistern, and the one which finally grants us a world, is also double. Bachelard points to the ambivalence of values surrounding every image of the subterranean world, and it is no different with the oneiric space of the cistern.[13] As the protecting place for her reverie, a place where she can see and not be seen, it represents a condensation of the most intimate forces of her desire. Although it is a man-made construction, the cistern becomes for Anna a kind if natural grotto because of the manner in which she inhabits it. Anna is intensely happy in her grotto. Making a small square with her hands, she imagines that the floor of the canal is "pasted and mashed flat with old circus banners and newspapers about 1936 and 1940 and the war and the movie star who died" (p. 272). The cistern thus becomes a kind of tomb of quotidian life which contains objects that the upper world has consumed. They have all been read, or seen, or discarded. They no longer demand a regard. In a sense, they too are "dead" and can be read without their meaning provoking anxiety.

The objects in the cistern have a passive quality about them which reflects human consciousness having passed through them functionally—gum wrappers and theater tickets and bus transfers,—but for Anna they are images which help to build up a world. The surprise of seeing the dead movie star, who would presumably solicit many admiring glances if alive, is that he (or she, the text does not specify anima or animus) could not be "resurrected" by any gaze. The famous movie star inhabits this world only as a forgotten phantom. These objects are haunted by a passivity, pasted and mashed flat as they are, but the impression is inescapable that Anna is actively *decorating* this space, making it pleasant for her sojourn with Frank in their papery existence when they rest during the dry seasons "dry and compact and old and quiet" (p. 272).[14] This very compacted existence hints at a potential for metamorphosis and blossoming in the rainy season which completes the natural cycle.

But if there are grottos of wonderment, then there are also grottos of fear (the word grotesque of course derives from grotto): "Upon the threshold [of the grotto] one can sense a synthesis of fright and amazement, a desire to enter and a fear of entering. It is here that the threshold takes on its values of grave decision."[15] We know that Anna has already made this decision to cross a fearful boundary; the narrator tells us that "she looked like she had made a decision" (p. 270) when she at first does not respond to her sister's denigrating remarks about her being born of a human mother and not being some kind of changeling. The grotto is a thinly disguised image of the womb. Only the crypt is less disguised, and Anna believes that the cistern is the place Frank has gone to die in a despairing attempt to escape his mother's moral interdictions (p. 271).

The thematic sequence cistern/grotto/crypt suggests a deeper, more prophetic underworld that echoes and doubles our being with images that may be frightful, but they do not end in a labyrinth of anguish where meaning cannot be found. As Bachelard points but, the images of the labyrinth stem from the imagination of difficult, anguished movement.[16] There is no suggestion of that in our story. Quite the contrary, as I have been at pains to point out. Anna says of the cistern: "It's empty and it echoes if you talk" (p. 272). When Anna had taken her bath earlier that morning, she had indeed heard Frank calling to her from deep within the cistern. It was then that she actually hallucinated a phallic eye staring at her. These events certainly touch on more disturbing fantasy levels, especially when Anna describes, to her sister's shocked outrage, soaping herself to hide herself, but Bradbury was right to excise them from the revised version of the story published in *The October Country* (1955). Anna's fantastic world is not the result of a Freudian splitting of the ego (*Spaltung*) or psychosis. Besides, these events happen in the morning, long before the experience of reverie which is integral in itself and not a narrative action related to them. But the text as it stands in *Dark Carnival* does lead the reader to speculate that when the imagination is repressed so strongly it tends to become perceptually uncanny or wholly other. Reverie on the other hand is not to be understood as a projected hallucination that is the result of repression. It is more than that because it offers us a humanized imaginary world.

Not only does the cistern protect love and repose, when filled with water it takes Anna and Frank on a journey down to the sea and eventually all over the world. In her reverie, their travelling will be "hand and hand, bobbing and floating, carefree and relaxed, down all the streets doing little crazy upright dances when they're caught in sudden swirls. . ." (p. 275). At this supernatural honeymoon, the anima and animus dance their happiness. Anna takes pleasure in naming every street they cross, with nobody in the upper world suspecting that they are there. As Bachelard indicates, the fantasy of inhabiting the grotto as a world *is* accompanied by the desire to see without being seen.[17] Nevertheless, this seeing is of a special kind belonging to reverie alone. What is "hurt and bleeding up in the outer world" (p. 273) cannot be experienced in the protected grotto. It is a world of dreaming observation, and the water even opens gently the eyes of the lovers so that they can see each other (p. 274). Fantastically, behind her beautiful blue eyelids, Anna reads the newspapers with closed eyes. Despite all of its descriptive passages, this world is meant to be situated on the far side of the visual field, as the reverse side of the represented city, as a "dead city" (p. 269).

Our response to this world leads us to reject the fear of fantasy manifested by Anna's sister, Juliet, her double-yet-opposite (and there may be a pun on cistern/ sisters). From the very beginning Juliet had tried to link Anna's reverie world with the objective world of cause and effect, a nightmare of determinism, corruption and decay. It is no wonder that Anna is finally forced to make a demand that her desire be recognized. In an explosion of bitter frustration, she ironically demands the real names of the anima and animus. Then subsiding in a sense of profound despair, she asks "Christ, Juliet, what good *are* we?"(p. 277). The question would simply be melodramatic did Anna not choose to die authentically later, as she had dreamed it, ending forever her futile life as an old maid. Although "Cistern" at times skirts sentimentality, it is ultimately saved by its nuanced exploration of the ontological paradoxes of idealized love. Anna remains a sympathetic character because of her prodigious dreaming in which she is mistress of all her doublings despite her sister's disapprobation. In "Cistern" we seem to have entered momentarily into that imaginary realm of significance between the unnameable and the named, where *many* words are required to materialize a fantastic world.

5

Reverie and Science Fiction

Although our study of reverie in Bradbury's fantasy texts is not directly concerned with the ideological implications of genre as such, in this chapter we will nevertheless discuss the Marxist-sociological SF criticism of Bradbury which we briefly referred to in the introduction (SF in the following discussion abbreviates "science fiction" only). As we indicated there, the reader's role in SF narration, as postulated by Darko Suvin, leaves no room for reverie. Curiously, however, Suvin does affirm that SF is a form of critical daydreaming which educates us to compare its possibilities with historical actuality.[.] Let us therefore now elaborate on this Marxist theory of the reading process, and then discern whether or not it accurately describes the experience of reverie in one of Bradbury's SF texts, "The Golden Apples of the Sun."

Suvin's theory of the reader's role in SF narration is presented mainly in one rather dense chapter of this theoretical *Metamorphoses of Science Fiction* entitled "SF and the Novum."[.] Suvin offers no complete readings (although there are some examples), so it is difficult to know at times exactly how the reader interacts with an SF text; nor is there any general theory of the text, despite the obvious structuralist bent of the argument. Basically, however, the theory involves two parameters: estrangement and cognition. Suvin's first internal determination of SF as a genre hinges on the notion of cognitive innovation (or *novum*) which introduces into the implied reader's norms an unknown dimension. It is not immediately clear from the text exactly what Suvin means by "implied reader." Sometimes he seems to refer to a real, sociologically defined reader and at other times to some kind of ideal reader. In any case, he does not discuss the role of images in the construction of meaning in the manner of Iser (any imagistic action of a text upon a reader would seem to imply his involvement with ideology). The postulated innovation, however, may be according to Suvin simply one discrete new invention (gadget, technique, relationship) or a complete change in spatio-temporal locus, but the postulation of this *novum* must be in accordance with the known paradigms of science. (Suvin's distinction between SF extrapolation as an extension of bourgeois ideology and valid SF as beging innovative and dealienating need not concern us here; nor need his questionable assertion that

Marx and Einstein together founded this new paradigm of science as an open-ended corpus of knowledge.) SF narration therefore rejects any supernatural or occult logic in its second reader aspect, validation.

If the effect of innovation is to estrange the implied reader's familiar conventions, validation of the novelty in a SF test is accomplished by leading the reader inexorably through scientifically methodical cognition. The reader has to be led to validate his discoveries in accordance with cognitive logic (something of the character of a scientific "thought-experiment" is intended here). Suvin provides no concrete reading demonstrating how a reader's interaction with an SF text creates this validation, although he does give the example of simulsequentialist physics in Le Guin's *The Dispossessed* as playing the role of scientific validation for certain plot events. Now the novelty in SF (to take one of the narrative consequences of the *novum*) supposedly shapes temporal and spatial relationships into "the spiral structures of valid SF." Again, Suvin provides no concrete reading for consideration; he simply states that Le Guin's Shevek, his physics, and the binary planetary sociopolitics and psychology of *The Dispossessed* create "a tale of a higher quality than the wish-dreams of, say, a Van Vogt, where all the obstacles are fake since the protagonist is a superman enforcing his will both on enemies and supposed allies."[3] Apparently, the latter type of narrative logic is, if not overt ideology, simply a stimulus for the reader's Freudian dream of aggressive power.

For Suvin, the presence of scientific cognition serves to differentiate SF from the "supernatural" genres of fantasy in the wider sense (called simply fantastic narratives by Rabkin—fairy tales, myths, horror stories, heroic fantasy, etc.), which do not allow scientific explanation, and from naturalistic fiction as well, which does not require it. But Bradbury's texts in particular belong to a misshapen (according to Suvin) sub-genre of real SF, "science-fantasy," which does not use scientific logic for validation, but only for an excuse or rationalization, or even a pretense that is abandoned later at the author's whim. Here, in providing an example of what SF is *not,* Suvin is a bit more concrete. Suvin asserts that Stevenson's *The Strange Case of Dr. Jekyll and Mr. Hyde* cheats in terms of its basic narrative logic by an unclear oscillation between science and fantasy. Suvin speculates that Stevenson wanted to write a moral allegory for readers who were no longer disposed to accept one presented in a straightforward way. Hence, the chemical concoction which transforms Jekyll into Hyde was an unrepeatable affair, and later Hyde returns without any chemical stimulus, by force of desire and habit. Although it may introduce estrangement from the familiar (fantastic events, in Rabkin's terminology) science-fantasy is therefore not fiction whose *novum* is cognitively validated. SF, in Suvin's axiomatic formulation, is to be distinguished from non-SF by the narrative dominance or hegemony of a fictional *novum* (novelty, innovation) validated by cognitive logic.

Suvin then proceeds to draw out the consequences of this cognitive-ideological distinction for narrative structure. The one which concerns us directly we have already touched upon, namely, the assertion that texts based on science-fantasy lead to narratives which are akin to myth because they return the universe to equilibrium and archaic order. Science-fantasy is, according to Suvin, who repeats the strictures of James Blish, a grateful abandonment of the life of the mind, which seems to consist for Suvin in open scientific plausibility and systematic speculation in a constantly moving framework of knowledge. SF narration must therefore entail a change in the whole universe of the tale. And the easiest and dominant narrative way of driving home a significant change of this nature is, according to Suvin, to have the hero grow into and with it (as in Lem's *Solaris* which deals with the whole problem of scientific inquiry) by using a protagonist who has to understand the *novum* for himself and for the reader. Instead of the additive or linear structure of the adventure tale, of the suspense or detective tale, valid SF evinces a spiral structure that transforms the entire universe of the tale.

Furthermore, the narrative consequences of the *novum* entail, according to Suvin, certain ontological effects. Suvin argues that in a naturalistic or realistic text (such as *Madame Bovary* where the violation of the norm is adultery) transgression of a cultural norm is merely cultural. The *novum* of SF is, however, more than merely cultural, it is ontological, brought about by an ontic change in a character's reality either because of displacement in space and/or time or because the reality around him changes. In valid SF, the actualized novum of space/time displacement causes the reader to search for the cognitive meaning of plot events which are estranging or defamiliarizing. SF may borrow some narrative patterns from mythography, but never the pattern of eternal return:

> SF's analogical historicity may or may not be mythomorphic, but—as I have argued in chapter 2—it cannot be mythopoetic in any sense except the most trivial one of possessing "a vast sweep" or "a sense of wonder": another superannuated slogan of much SF criticism due for a deserved retirement into the same limbo as extrapolation. For myth is reenactment, eternal return, and the opposite of a creative human freedom.[4]

In spite of the theoretical sophistication of Suvin's poetics of SF, his theory of myth belongs really to a long tradition of reductive, orthodox Marxist interpretations of literature, which argue that art historically arises out of primitive magic. One can sympathize with his insistence that novelty, to be aesthetically valid, has to lead the reader to exercise his own cognitive powers—we have asserted the same for fantasy texts based on the reader's reverie—but is myth always mystification? According to the tradition to which Suvin belongs, myth is the transposition of material social conditions and the actual phenomena and conflicts of our time into a timeless reality, into a changeless, original state of being. Myth in the context of Marxist criticism is almost a synonym for a "magical" ideology which serves to justify the status quo. Eternal cycles of nature, human essences, or the idea of a collective unconscious functioning through archetypes:

these have always been anathema to the usual Marxist view of literature (and man) as variably determined by material social conditions. Although Suvin does leave some room for mythopoetic patterns that might cause us to reflect on our existence, he seems to denigrate them as well. Perhaps he wishes to distinguish himself from archetypal critics such as Northrop Frye who assert that SF is a modern displacement of romance. In Frye's view, the essential effect of romance is imagined awe and wonder, and this genre in particular carries the ontological significance of being man's vision of his own life as quest for identity. But even in Frye, the theory of imagery is static and patterned, if not ideological.

Now, I can agree with Suvin that the study of SF as a genre should grow beyond the simple demonstration of how a particular story invites the exercise of imagined awe and wonder, even though these responses are recognized by phenomenological thinkers as the beginning of the reflective life. For the sake of argument, I can even go along with him when he asserts that Bradbury's texts are science-fantasy and not valid SF. His viewpoint seems to be held logically and consistently. I cannot, however, agree with the conclusions he draws from the matrix of these distinctions concerning ideology—or that Bradbury's text epitomize human unfreedom and the willing surrender of the mind to some archaic mystical fog. Granted, Bradbury's science-fantasy (particularly *The Martian Chronicles* which bears no resemblance to the known scientific facts about Mars, except that it is the next planet out from the sun after Earth) does not evince the narrative dominance of a fictional novum validated by cognitive logic. But does this necessarily mean that because Bradbury uses a variety of mythopoetic thought (more percisely, the oneiric logic of invention peculiar to reverie) that he seeks solely to plunge the reader's consciousness into the inchoate and the inarticulate? Is reverie more or less ideological, not ontological, and unchecked by any cognition?

I think that Suvin's view of the reader's role in fantasy texts can be shown to be narrowly generic. A phenomenological view of the text affirms that although generic demands and expectations are relevant, the reader's role will be different in each text. The unique role of the reader must be taken into account if we are to avoid the pitfalls of generic criticism; and if we are to assess the cognitive demands of a text without labeling it beforehand as ideology. A thorough study of the relationship between reverie and ideology is beyond the scope of this study, but I might note in passing that French critics have discovered in Bradbury's "inconsistencies" that the text was directing them to surrealist imaginings—or even to *sur*rational imaginings (a phrase of Bachelard's that Breton was fond of). For these critics, Bradbury demonstrates every confidence in open reason, imaginative freedom, and social progress. But actually, Suvin's logic-chopping approach to genre can be shown not to have gone far enough. In accusing Bradbury of irrationalism and sloppy science, he himself overlooks a theoretical generic possibility (yet his system, as a deductive one, claims to be complete), that is, SF narration which is *not* supernatural and *not* naturalistic yet which is highly cognitive without the use of scientific validation.

At first glance, this negation of a negation may seem to be nothing more than the return of the monstrous and misshapen genre of science-fantasy, yet there is a crucial positive difference—the presence of a fantasy which is cognitive. Is Suvin's assumption about Bradbury's science-fantasy valid?

Quite apart from an inadequacy to deal with the imaginary world in reading in other than reductive terms (see, for example, Suvin's own account of the space and time of the implied reader presented in section 2.4 of "SF and the Novum"), a chief objection to this theory is its undialectical exclusion of fantasy from the domain of the cognitive. We have already mentioned in chapter 2 the cognitive and historical truth-value of fantasy images according to another Marxist philosopher (and one who understands the value of negation), Herbert Marcuse. "The Golden Apples of the Sun" (1953) manifests something of the optimistic thesis of *Eros and Civilization* (1955), for in it Bradbury sees technology transforming the destructive dialectics of Eros and Thanatos into a civilization of aesthetic sensuousness and freedom. Furthermore, the vehicle of this liberation is the play impulse—a child's oneiric dream of capturing the energy of the sun to transform in one gigantic leap the historical labor of mankind. Obliquely, it refers to the problem of the atomic bomb and the frightening possibility of mankind's destruction of civilization. It accomplishes its world largely through the activation of material images of childhood. These images contain for the Captain of the mission a revival of repressed memories of gratifications and an Orphic song he once composed that united play, peace, and salvation in a world where the golden apples of being were accessible to mankind. As we shall see, the Captain is a kind of Prometheus figure, and it is through his transformative experience that we come to know the significance of the *novum* in this story. Let us briefly indicate what that innovation is.

For Marcuse, Prometheus was not the Father-God-Establishment-defying myth of Karl Marx, he was rather the archetype-hero of the performance principle (the socio-historical mode of the reality principle), a hero who creates culture at the price of perpetual pain. He further symbolized productiveness, the unceasing effort to master life, but in his productivity, blessing and curse, progress and toil, are inextricably entwined. He is therefore very much assigned by Marcuse to the sphere of labor and production that lies outside of play. Bradbury's *"novum"* (besides that of the spaceship and the spatio-temporal displacement of the hero which we will come to in a moment) is to transform this cognitive culture hero into a child at play who symbolizes the other sphere of aesthetic sensuousness and freedom that Marcuse identified as utopian. Once we understand this cognitive dimension of "The Golden Apples of the Sun," we will have no trouble understanding the narrative logic of the story and the oneiric transformations of it. In essence, Bradbury transforms and softens the toil of Prometheus through the projection of the archetype of the child. Our oneiric reading method is therefore all the more necessary here because it is only by becoming sensitive to the archetype in dreaming while reading that we can properly assess the imaginative *and* cognitive demands of the story, which concern the meaning of existence, and because framed within the narrative is the poetic meaning of why we undertake the journey at all. All this can only be recovered through reverie, for the text explicitly asks the reader to equate the experience of the mission with a child's grasping of a handful of flowers on a homeward walk from school.

I have chose this story also because it contains a theme still central to Bradbury's imagination: the romance of space exploration and the necessity of mankind's quest for knowledge of the cosmos. "The Golden Apples of the Sun" is a highly mythopoetic text, invoking the myth of Prometheus, among others, in order to suggest a meaning for the mission it describes. The plot involves a handful of men, in a specially-equipped rocketship, whose mission is to bring back to earth a part of the sun which will feed all of humanity with its energy. The Captain of this crew embodies that pioneering spirit of "knowledge at all costs" typical of astronaut characters in modern SF (initially, at least, he embodies that spirit of domination found by Marcuse in the Prometheus myth). Yet the story offers, I think, irrefutable proof of Bradbury's confidence in the dialectical progress of reason and wonder, for while we are meant to become intimately aware of the functioning of our childhood imagination, we are also led in this way to discover deficiencies in the dominant thought systems of our society. Is there a happier world of childhood reverie dwelling within us, a world of slow and easy time waiting to be awakened? And if so, how is it possible to integrate the feelings of the child, his sense of novelty and wonder at appearances (the archetype of the child is, we should remember, a reservoir of enthusiasm for life in all its manifold possibilities) into the complex intellectual powers of adulthood caught within the existential frame of the human condition? Will we survive the destructive invention of the atom bomb? Can technology transform the Freudian instinctual dialectic to which Marcuse refers? These are questions that Bradbury wrestles with so pertinaciously in this mythopoetic work, questions raised for him by the human drama in contemporary America which was becoming history as he was responding to it.

Of course, I am not saying that we recover here the personality or worldview of the author—even if that were possible from the reading of one text, to do it would be an exercise in reduction—but rather the fundamental concern which motivates the text: in short, the question that it seeks to answer and that it poses again and again to its interpreters. "The Golden Apples of the Sun" in fact stimulates this cognitive activity by a game of quotations from past literature (and some of these texts are not fantasy at all, hence the falsity of generic distinction made by Suvin and others whose poetic does not include the idea of a functioning repertoire) that buoys the reader in the back-and-forth hermeneutical movement that constitutes the meaning of the story.

This is a very clear example of a way in which a science-fantasy text "plays with possibilities" that are highly cognitive yet not necessarily scientific, and we will show how it functions later. For the moment, let me remind the reader that I have argued in the introduction that Bachelard's reading while dreaming *(lire en rêvant)* was intended to interpret fantasy texts by the dreams we have in reading the text, thus restoring to us our sense of the autonomy of imaginative production (and therefore its ability to correct deficient realities) that the fantasy genre requires. I also affirmed that this type of reading would allow us to make thematic the oneiric logic of invention in a story. Nevertheless, I amended this reading method to include the historical dimension of Iser's repertoire. I will now argue that Bradbury's strategy in "The Golden Apples of the Sun" is to transform then-popular notions of existentialism and Freudian culture-criticism by having the reader explore a certain phenomenological structure of imaginative consciousness, namely, reverie towards childhood *(rêverie vers l'enfance).* We will now discuss this structure of consciousnes together with other elements of the repertoire which make up the implied reader portrait.

The structure of consciousness embodied in "The Golden Apples of the Sun" is highly complex and exemplifies, indeed, the most intricate kind of imaginative transformation of self and world that Bachelard discusses in *The Poetics of Reverie.*[9] This structure tends to mingle memory and imagination in an inextricable fashion and involves a reaching backward in time from the standpoint of adulthood toward object and cosmic reveries we may have had as a child, reactivating and reimagining these structures. Bachelard's felicitous phrase, *rêverie vers l'enfance,* is designed to indicate his special ontology of childhood, so different from the being-towards-death school of the existentialists, and equally different from Freudian analyses of childhood which argue that our imaginative life is to a large extent *determined* by real childhood experiences in the context of the family. Bachelard's ontological inquiry into childhood is concerned with general structures that, as *possibilities,* pervade human existence. In this sense he affirms that a potential childhood is within all of us, and we will see that Bradbury, while recognizing the Freudian theme of lost infancy, the golden age, and paradise, follows much more closely this Bachelardian ontology in his mode of fantasy. Bachelard affirms that when we go looking for this potential childhood in our reveries, we relive it even more in its very possibilities than in its reality. But Bachelard is quick to remind us that this type of reverie is a definite existential concern, and is not something we can attain from the perspective of adulthood without an openness to the possibilities of childhood.

The reverie towards childhood may be blocked by various culture complexes. These anthropocosmic complexes of Jungian fantasy can, if properly imagined and understood in their archetypal aspect, provide a counterbalancing response to elements of the dominant thought system which excludes the phenomenology of astonishment or wonder. Bachelard offers us some suggestions about how the existential confrontation with these archetypes might be successful: "In order to rediscover the language of fables, it is necessary to participate in the existentialism of the fabulous, to become body and soul an admiring being and replace perception of the world with admiration."[10] This passage suggests a participatory mode of reading, a total acceptance of an archetypal world entered into on its own terms rather than a search for origins: *retrouver* is used in the original French in the sense of rediscovering the use of childhood reverie for oneself. This experience can also be, in keeping with our revision of Bachelard, the experience of a character in a fantasy fiction. It may form part of the *"novum"* experience that he has to come to terms with in a science-fantasy text — at least that is what I want to argue here.

When successful, this type of reverie is marked, according to Bachelard, by a recovery of the language of fables, the original childhood fables that we composed in solitude, for ourselves. It is characteristic of the existential fabulous to take the world given by perception and translate it into a realm of fantasy, as children often do in Bradbury's stories, imagining that some wrinkle-faced-old crone is indeed a witch from foreign lands. In all his writing, Bradbury is sensitive to the ways in which childhood imagination can irradiate the commonplace with an aura of romance; as existential fabulist, he finds it difficult to accept inadequacies and oppressions of the social system.

In this story he uses the existential fabulous for an oneiric criticism of society (as in *Fahrenheit 451*, the subject of our next chapter, where it is developed at length) that reminds us of the ontological possibilities of childhood. In Bachelard's ontology of childhood, which Bradbury largely follows, *angst* or anxiety is not the most general structure in which the world (including the social dimension of existence with others, the *Mitwelt*) is revealed to us. The child in reverie has hardly yet taken up the task of confronting non-being or the spatial thrownness of existence, being-there. And, according to Bachelard, the time of childhood is of the primary and story-book coloring of the seasons, the very memory of our belonging to the world. Childhood is a being-*for*-the-world, as he playfully remarks.

Formulated in Bachelard's phrase *(rêverie vers l'enfance)* is also an indication of direction; in fact, an oneiric direction in which the consciousness of a reader/dreamer would return, following the path opened by the image, to a happier world of mingled memory and imagination outside the responsibilities of the adult world: "In our reverie which imagines while remembering, our past takes on substance again."[11] Further, there is a tension set up in consciousness, when we are called toward this region of being, which we interpret as an attempt to detemporalize the narrative process and its concatenation of dramatic events. Bachelard writes: "When the poets call us toward this region, we know a tender reverie, a reverie hypnotized by the faraway."[12] The well-loved image remembered from childhood needs a special, we might even say cumulative or vertical, time to develop. The image gives to words the slow time needed for dreaming, for reverie. Conversely, images are animated in the presence of certain words.

This is expressed in a quite lovely manner in "The Golden Apples of the Sun." When the Captain speaks, the words in his mouth have an imaginary climate and substance: the word "North" dissolves slowly on his tongue like a bit of ice cream. A truly successful reverie towards childhood vanquishes and transforms parental or anthropocosmic complexes opposed to happy reverie, and becomes a cosmic or world reverie. The dreaming child wants to be at home in the world he imagines, in his own special relation to the world. Often this happiness is expressed in oral images. The world is an immense fruit which we eat; there is nothing in it which is alien or harmful to us; we nourish ourselves on the world. We shall explore more fully the reverberations of images in this reverie in a moment, but first we need to indicate what further structuring factors will come into play (as a part of the text's repertoire) during our reading and produce the poignant tension to which Bachelard refers.

In the Freudian historical schema, the development of control over fire and the making of it into the supreme cultural object involves the renunciation of instinctual pleasure and the concomitant development of highly complex ego functions; always there is required a delicate balance of control, a mastery of instinct governing the ability to conserve, confine, extinguish and reilluminate fire.[13] The myths surrounding the acquisition of fire usually indicate that some kind of trick is necessary, and this generates most of the narrative logic of events. Furthermore, in the Freudian schema of civilization and its discontents, the god who is defrauded is the id and its pleasure principle. Critics of fantasy such as Rabkin see in the Prometheus myth the story of western civilization's consistently felt fear of the power conferred on it by increasing knowledge.[14] According to Rabkin, the myth symbolically handles our fears for us. Because Prometheus suffers daily for our sins, Rabkin argues, the sin of our having fire, as well as the guilt for fires gone out of control, belongs to Prometheus, not us. One senses in Rabkin's argument the psychoanalytic view of our response to literature. The formal structure of the work is used by us as a means of defense. This obviates in turn the necessity for us to grapple with any unpleasant implications of such fantasies. We shift the responsibility onto literature. Thus our psyche, by investing its desire in literature, gets a return in the form of freedom from self-control. This view of the reader's role in fantasy is so simple that one can sympathize with Marxist critics such as Suvin who mistakenly disparage myth; literature in this view is at best consolation, at worst an evasion of self-knowledge; it offers little that is cognitive.

For this part, Bachelard briefly describes the action of the Prometheus complex in *The Psychoanalysis of Fire* as comprising all the psychic tendencies which drive us to know as much as our fathers, more than our fathers.[15] It designates both the will to intellectuality and the interdictions forbidding it, and it is the "Oedipus complex" of the child's intellectual life. Furthermore, it is only by *handling* the forbidden object (in this case fire, a dangerous one) that we can prove and perfect our knowledge and superiority, rediscovering in the process our primordial relationship to the universe in material imagination. Thus the problem for the child is one of clever disobedience in seizing fire for his own reverie. From this point of view, "The Golden Apples of the Sun" negotiates the prohibitions against playing with fire by a series of negations and dynamic inversions expressed by images of intense heat and cold.

As we shall see, this is the oneiric logic of invention in the story. In order to transform imaginatively the overt narrative level, as readers we also must achieve the theft and reappropriation of the pleasure object. When the fire is drawn up into the body of the spaceship and contained or bound, we are able to draw on the power of this magically transformative action for an imaginative flight of sublimating images which finally allows the resonant image of the child in cosmic reverie to appear in the mind of the Captain. This highly conscious and aesthetic kind of incorporation involving the whole body keeps the reverie substance separate yet accessible to the self as a stable source of pleasure.

On the oneiric level, the level of material imagination, the text allows us to participate in the interior life of matter before the interdictions of the Prometheus complex (outside the sphere of the performance principle in Marcuse's terms). Thus, as the text shuttles back and forth between the terror and wonder of the Promethean task of scooping out, from the inside of a fantastic super-cooled rocketship, a bit of the "flesh of God" (which in a significant passage is referred to as a maternal substance), and the repose offered by images from childhood, we are stimulated to constitute the existential fabulous, the aspect of archetypal imagination under which the narrative events of the story are to be imagined.

This quest story is to be imagined in part under the sign of the child, as the way a child might attempt such a journey—hence the fabulous exaggeration we find in certain of its images (packing along two-thousand sour lemonades and a thousand white-capped beers for this journey to the wide Sahara). But our journey through this series of imaginative negations will not be without its price. Mortality resides in this existentialism of the fabulous, revealed when death silently erupts on the crew. As a result of blind chance—the structural imperfections of a space suit—one of the members of the crew is frozen to death. This mechanical failure (one of the possibilities of *things,* not consciousness) is viewed from an adult perspective, as part of the unreasonableness of the world.

This sudden estrangement from a familiar world, in which we feel ourselves as exiles deprived of the memory of a lost home or the hope of a promised land, this divorce between man and his life, was basic to the sensitivity of the absurd widespread in post-World War II existentialist fiction.[6] But science fiction seems to have arrived at the existential position relatively independently.[7] "The Golden

Apples of the Sun'' tells us that even in a universe deserted by God or meaning, man must struggle to remain human. Working within the conventions of science fiction's qualified rationalism, Bradbury imagines a voyage through space as an existential situation. There are no signposts to guide us, no North or South, we are faced with absolute annihilation from the sun and black space threatens to swallow us without a trace.

These absolute forbidding qualities of time and space admittedly have little to do with Einsteinian theory, but accompanying the plot is a dialogue between the Captain and his crew which takes the form of excited questions and answers calculated to launch the reader in the process of acculturation itself. Through the authors' names and the titles of their books, the dialogue pre-structures our response by providing us with schemata that aid us as we search for a solution to the problem that the text poses (the meaning of the mission, in human terms). Naturally, since the narrative, the oneiric and to a degree the Freudian fantasy of oral incorporation, suggested perhaps as early as the title—since all these textual levels interact during the reading process, other readers will no doubt transform the story somewhat differently. In this analysis I have been concerned to indicate passages where the reader's role is to transform narrative fact into the oneiric possibilities through dialectical sublimation.

We are already in the midst of tension between the narrative and oneiric levels in the opening dialogue of the story. The Captain gives the direction "South" (traveling down towards the sun) and the crew responds in consternation with the scientific answer, hoping to validate scientifically their existential situation: " 'But,' said his crew, 'there simply *aren't* any directions out here in space' " (p. 164).[18] This initial information at once gives us a location and a lack of it. Since ordinary space is negated, we must search for something else. The Captain affirms the oneiric direction of the mission, already deep in his own reverie where words have their own climate and dream themselves:

> "When you travel on down toward the sun," replied the captain, "and everything gets yellow and warm and lazy, then you're going in one direction only." He shut his eyes and thought about the smouldering, warm, faraway land, his breath moving gently in his mouth. "South." He nodded slowly to himself. "South." (p. 164)

Invariably, as in "Cistern," a character's reverie is described as beginning outside the visual field. We may expect that soon the Captain's reverie will activate certain archetypal figures or situations of the collective unconscious.

In the next paragraph, we learn that the ship has several names, at least two of which are mythical: *Copa de Oro* (introducing a flower image which returns later as a synthesizing image of the entire experience of the imaginary in this text), *Prometheus* and *Icarus*. These last two mythical names, as a functional part of the text's repertoire, aid the reader in constructing a reference point for the meaning of the mission. *Icarus* suggests its dangers, *Prometheus* its task, and *Copa de*

Oro (cup of gold), the Spanish name for a flower, gives us a word-image for reverie which makes poetic the imaginary response to the *novum* that is developing. On the oneiric level, the game of quotations from literature leaves open paths of reverie into the imaginary worlds of other texts concerned with the problem of the child's relation to the fabulous:

> And now as the sun boiled up at them they remembered a score of verses and quotations:
> " 'The golden apples of the sun'?"
> "Yeats."
> " 'Fear no more the heat of the sun'?"
> "Shakespeare, of course!"
> " 'Cup of Cold'? Steinbeck. 'The Crock of Gold'? Stephens. And what about the pot of gold at the rainbow's end? *There's* a name for our trajectory, by God. Rainbow!"
> "Temperature?"
> "One thousand degrees Fahrenheit!" (p. 165)

The text begins to quote the fantastic temperatures within the ship, but not before giving us a grounding in literary history and an aid to help us imagine the rainbow trajectory of the reverie. The text's repertoire offers us a spectrum of previous solutions to the problem of man's existence and especially his relationship to a childhood universe. A stream of molten gold seems to run through these quotations, activating the reader's imagination to fill out the other verses and quotations that are not mentioned specifically. This activity creates a fusion of historical horizons that evokes the fascination and risk that a player involved in a game experiences as he plays with possibilities, one of which he must choose and carry out. In addition to its meaning of a group of twenty items, the word score can indicate a game or contest (a record of points scored or gained), a musical composition, or generally to achieve or win, to leave a scratch on the surface of anonymity; all of these meanings are, I think, active here. Let us examine two of the quotations, perhaps less familiar to some readers, for some of these aspects.

James Stephen's *The Crock of Gold,* for example, is an apocalyptic fantasy full of song in the Irish manner, after Blake. On one level it is an allegory of the human faculties, dislocated in a philosopher's shadowy forest at the outset, but united at the end in a triumphant sunlit return of the dancing pagan gods to Ireland. Caitlin, the central female character who represents mankind's emotional nature, learns that true happiness means to unite the knowledge of adulthood with the gaiety of the child. Stephens exhorts the reader at the end of this novel with Blakean rhetoric to come away and quench his heart's desire in a fantasy world where all the human powers are in balance (and the leprechauns have their pot of gold to ransom themselves from evil.) The pot of gold itself might stand as a symbol for the wealth of the imaginary field of experience in reading—intangible but always within our reach when we need it, as Iser has written. [9] Steinbeck's historical novel, *Cup of Gold,* the fictional biography of the pirate Henry Morgan, also has as its central theme the problem of uniting the child's heart with the man's mind. Young Henry Morgan's dream of becoming a great man and a pirate (first introduced to the reader through a fireside reverie) is symbolized by the Cup of Gold, and he single-mindedly directs all his energies, and risks his life in numerous games and adventures, to accomplish his quest. But when he finally does sack the seemingly inviolable city of Panama (known as The Cup of Gold) with his buccaneers, after a bloody battle in which he kills his best friend, he discovers that his dream has vanished, reduced to a tawdry real cup of gold that he finds in the loot taken from the city. In Steinbeck's novel, Henry Morgan is unable to unite his naive dreams with the civilization he has to face. He sells out his dream and becomes the respected and secure governor of Jamaica. Bradbury uses Yeats and Shakespeare as further climates of the same word. In this manner, the text evokes a shared heritage of allusions to aid the reader at the very outset of the story.

The imaginative climates of the text emerge in the following paragraph, with its balancing of frost and fire:

> The captain stared from the huge dark-lensed port, and there indeed was the sun, and to go to that sun and touch it and steal part of it forever away was his quiet and single idea. In this ship were combined the cooly delicate and the coldly practical. Through corridors of ice and milk-frost, ammoniated winter and storming snowflakes blew. Any spark from that vast hearth burning out there beyond the callous hull of this ship, any small firebreath that might seep through would find winter, slumbering here like all the coldest hours of February. (p. 165)

From this passage, which poeticizes sensation and substance, oneiric criticism can discern the emergence of the Promctheus complex: "...to go to that sun and touch it and steal part of it forever away was his quiet and single idea." In order to inhabit this dream of touching the sun, the Captain as child first cleverly renounces fire by inhabiting corridors of frost. He imagines a pure climate of childhood, a condensation of all the coldest hours of winter. February is absolute, yet humanized cold, a season that protects the dreamer from any "spark" or germ of any other reverie that might interfere with his quiet and single idea. In the scientific view of thermodynamics we know, of course, that cold is merely the absence of heat. And the means for attaining our goal is a fairly realistic spaceship which embodies the sterile purity of technology. But the narrative and oneiric levels interpenetrate. Ammoniated winter slumbers in repose and would contain any warming breath that tried to melt it.

Following the dynamism of the oneiric images, we learn that cold is a force in itself that the imagination uses to expel heat. Further complicating and complementing this oneiric tension is the fact that inside the super-cold world of the rocket the men are protected by insulating suits (which also protects the poet/Captain's warming breath), another variation on the theme of dynamic containment prominent in the story. The passage offers us several layers of significance, just as in our example from Poe in the introduction. We can thus understand why the statement of the Prometheus complex is itself framed by the narrator within description of the cooly delicate and the coldly practical. The oneiric is linked to narrative events but only as a means of enabling us to inhabit a world, however dangerous that may be (and however it may transform a more disturbing unconscious fantasy).

Even on the level of plot, where the narrative direction of the story is toward the real sun, and the Captain and crew are in danger of being killed, there are oneiric strategies. A surrealistic thermometer creates suspense by periodically speaking (and as desire gets closer to fulfillment it seems to shout or even scream) the outside temperature in degrees Fahrenheit, as if it could feel the struggle of the two climates at the approach of the oneiric source. This type of quotation or scoring (in the sense of making a mark that indicates position) uses a scientific scale, is a valid measure of the real temperature, but it is nevertheless a measure of reverie-excitement. It incites the reader to respond on the level of action, and to imagine the fantastic and fearful temperatures from within the arctic silence of the ship, as it touches the sun. In the following passage, an element from the narrative level of the text is juxtaposed with the instantaneous moment of the image which opens the path to a reverie-world again. The Captain speaks with all the quietness of the journey in his voice:

> "Now, we are touching the sun."
> Their eyes, thinking it, were melted gold. (p. 165)

In order to bridge this gap between fact and imaginative consciousness, dreamer and image, reading subject and world, must be interrelated on the same level of being. We search for an integrative dimension, an emotive-cognitive synthesis of meaning. The resulting image condenses for us the "long quietness" of the reverie up to this point. Now the collective vision of the Captain and crew is melted into an almost alchemical substance which expresses the admiring being, the shared enrichment of them all. Gold is at once their admiration and their pride at seeing the big and beautiful sun, and a reciprocal look between them and the world. This imaginative seeing in which the sun itself becomes a reverie object is nevertheless very much outside the visual field, behind a huge dark-lensed port where reverie is safe. Its meaning emerges as the reverse side of the represented world, as a negation of it. This is, of course, for the reader the experience of the imaginary. And if we consider the role of the material imagination here, we discover that it is the *touching* of the sun which activates the image. Furthermore, their eyes are *thinking* it, not merely passively registering its presence.

Though dreaming further on this image of melted gold, the reader gains access to a realm of the fabulous, a land of conquest and plunder beyond the rainbow. If we dwelt too long with this image we would find a reverie that would unloosen the thread of narrative, satisfying our recessive desires in heroic fantasy. Or retrospectively, we could imagine the long quietness of the journey through space which prepared this moment. But the narrator quickly casts us into another absolute situation before we have a chance to turn resonance into reverberation. A crew member asks what time it is. Everyone smiles at the absurdity of this question:

> For now there was only the sun and the sun and the sun. It was every horizon, it was every direction. It burned the minutes, the seconds, the hourglasses, the clocks; it burned all time and eternity away. It burned the eyelids and the serum of the dark world behind the lids, the retina, the hidden brain; and it burned sleep and the sweet memories of sleep and cool nightfall. (p. 165)

If there is such a thing as a naked confrontation with an archetype then this must be what it is. Fire has brought about an apocalypse of the body, having burnt away the entire length of the eye's pathway to the visual field, from the serum of the dark world behind the lids (the reverie-world of sublimation) through the hidden brain to human temporality itself. There no longer is any horizon, any world, or place where consciousness might find repose in a beautiful image. Meaning consists in the repetition of the word sun which drives out other meanings with its killing presence. Sometimes a little absence of meaning is necessary to dream freely and well.

The fulfillment of desire and reverie, the touching of the sun, will bring death into the crew in the next passage, as the ship itself begins to melt. This in turn activates a reverie towards childhood in the mind of the Captain which restores a human world. Paradoxically, however, although one man will be killed for breaking the interdiction, it will be from cold. Because of a structural imperfection in his suit, Bretton, the first mate, is frozen to death. The image of death's presence is a kind of frozen milk, a maternal substance which no longer nourishes life:

> Bretton, the first mate, fell flat to the winter deck. His protective suit whistled where, burst open, his warmness, his oxygen, and his life bloomed out in a frosted steam.
> "Quick!"
> Inside Bretton's plastic face-mask, milk crystals had already gathered in blind patterns. They bent to see.
> "A structural defect in his suit, Captain. Dead."
> "Frozen."
> They stared at that other thermometer which showed how winter lived in this snowing ship. One thousand degrees below zero. The captain gazed down upon the frosted statue and the twinkling crystals that iced over it as he watched. Irony of the coolest sort, he thought; a man afraid of fire and killed by frost. (p. 166)

But quite apart from its oneiric images of frosted steam, this passage bears a certain intellectuality that goes beyond the obvious ironies. Bradbury stages the scene so that the reader is forced to see the essential impersonality of death that technological failure can reveal. The blind patterns on Bretton's face-mask are also brute facts. And the irruption of death caused by the structural imperfection of a space suit tells us that we do belong to the realm of necessity. Yet these facts have to be imagined if they are to have human meaning. In other words the reader is led to formulate the meaning of this death through a series of perspectives that change even between sentences. The crew looks from the dead body to the other thermometer which shows how winter *lives* before it gives the scientific answer (to be precise, absolute zero is -459.67° Fahrenheit and not -1000 °F) to their gaze. Does scientific accuracy about the temperature within the ship really give us understanding? Bradbury seems to be saying that we do not necessarily escape a confrontation with the absurd because of the refinement of technology; in fact, our existential freedom and problems are only reflected back to us in an inverted and more paradoxical form when technology fails.

However, the blind pattern of Bretton's death will be compensated for at the end of the story when the ship returns to earth with an "unborn child" of fire in the womb of the ship (p. 169), but at this moment in the plot, there is no time to tend to Bretton's body—the ship itself has begun to melt (like an icicle, the narrator tells us, establishing an oneiric equivalent that will develop in the next sequence) because of a mechanical failure of a refrigeration pump. The Captain and his crew are all facing imminent death. The Captain jerks his head upward, sees the ceiling melting, and finds himself located in a region of reimagined childhood memories, pure memories which have no anxiety, but only a season:

> As if a motion-picture projector had jammed a single clear memory frame in his head, he found his mind focused ridiculously on a scene whipped out of childhood.
> Spring mornings as a boy he found he had leaned from his bedroom window into the snow-smelling air to see the sun sparkle the last icicle of winter. A dripping of white wine, the blood of cool but warming April fell from that clear crystal blade. Minute by minute, December's weapon grew less dangerous. And then at last the icicle fell with the sound of a single chime to the graveled walk below. (p. 166)

This experience of finding one's mind ridiculously focused on a scene is reminiscent of Camus' famous description of the absurd: the gestures of a man talking on the telephone behind a glass partition suddenly become mechanical, a meaningless pantomime, and the feeling of absurdity spreads to the world. But the "clear memory frame" whipped out of childhood is not, strictly speaking, a memory at all. It is the awakening consciousness of childhood reimagined and remembered in terms of its reverie. At first glance, this memory might seem completely kinetic and mechanical. Men, too, secrete the mechanical, as we remember from Camus. The picture seems cinematic (to follow the simile) and external to the consciousness which sees it. But if we examine the direct images of matter in this text, we are drawn into the glimmers of an intimate crossing of boundaries between the two climates. The boy finds himself leaning out from within an enclosed space to discover the world and his own consciousness of it at the same time. Here we can observe a spontaneous natural myth forming around the combat of the seasons, expressed in the phrases "December's weapon" and "April's blood." This image of the melting icicle, which is also the ship itself, is a grounding in the imaginative experience of matter and tries to draw us, and the Captain, into the solitude and security of a cosmic reverie where we would rediscover the language of fables. In Bachelardian terms, the Captain is indeed hypnotized by a faraway region. The references to "December's weapon" and "crystal blade" suggest a mythical world of childhood fantasy. He has entered, if only briefly, into the different ontological time of reverie, and he will have to integrate this rediscovery of childhood reverie into his adult experience a bit later on in the story.

But for now we can observe that the reader discovers that both climates of the story in fact block a happy reverie. The ice and snow of winter possess an absolute exteriority, the pure apparition of a hostile non-self; nor could a dreamer interiorize the annihilating sun. But with the mixing of the seasons of spring, a dynamic inversion takes place in the interior of substance. Active inside the cold, slumbering in repose, is heat. Both white wine and the blood of cool but warming April are interior substances becoming less and less dangerous for a dreamer. This is a reverie of substance, of the repeated, durational time of many spring mornings. The seasons of childhood, which were in such conflict with each other, are mixing. There is a wounding, a sense of existence trying itself out in a world increasingly commanded by the sun. But the child's consciousness has not yet taken upon itself the task of confronting non-being. The deliquescence of the icicle is the *matter* of this ontological condition which has nuances of both being and non-being. So the clear memory frame is a photograph, aesthetically composed, but reverie has provided the time and light for the picture to be ample. It has given duration and beauty to this image confided to memory, which the melting ship has just now activated.

In this manner, in the astonishment of the moment, the Captain is drawn out of the forward movement of events occurring in the ship towards the memory of an old childhood reverie. This detemporalization of the narrative process cannot, of course, stop the "film" from running for long. As the ship loses more refrigeration, the Captain is assailed by images of the future: he and his crew are ants in a flaming matchbox, space would drown out their screams like a black mossed well. Needless to say, these images, one of being burnt up in a kind of super-consciousness and the other of falling into unconsciousness, are too strong for the dreaming child, now forgotten by the Captain. Although they do not convey the anxiety of complete annihilation in space, because of their great fear we cannot enter into them for long: "...we're used to more leisurely dyings, measured in minutes and hours" (p. 167). But the Captain resolutely chooses to go ahead with the mission and confront these possibilities.

The next narrative sequence is crucial, involving the operation of the gigantic fantasmatic hand which holds the Cup. If the Captain is Prometheus about to seal fire, and if Bretton was Icarus who realized one possibility of this mission, then *Copa de Oro,* Cup of Gold, provides the archetypal mediation of reverie between these two extremes. The Captain operates it from within a robot glove. This highly coordinated work is a product of the developed rationality of consciousness and technology (based on renunciation of instinct), but we should remember that for the Prometheus complex the crucial moment is the handling of one's own fire. There is already an oneiric movement in the way the gigantic hand magnifies the slightest twitch of the Captain's hand, providing a "tremendous image of his own gesture" (p. 168). The text gives us the imaginary double of the hand, immediately translating us to the oneiric level of the text, offering the Captain the instantaneous fulfillment of his desire. Above all we note that it is a *beautiful* hand (whose Cup is named after a flower, in fact) which, once it has gotten the gift of fire, drips yellow flowers and white stars (p. 168). These images are produced from a beauty that is excess, from a realm outside labor and toil, beyond the streamlined economy of technology. Furthermore, in this dream of a hand touching the body and flesh of creative matter, of stealing solar light and a bit of divine intelligence, the Captain's Prometheus complex is transformed, sublimated, even as he draws this fire up into the body of his ship.

The archetypal image of the human heart and its desires, the Cup, now contains the gift that might burn forever. If, as Bachelard suggests, the Prometheus complex is the Oedipus complex of intellectual life, then the wish to be the father of one's own reverie is here fulfilled. The sun's flesh is the ultimate matter, the golden fruit of an imaginary world. It is also a maternal substance which "set out and mothered a galaxy" long ago (p. 168). According to the oneiric logic here, which is by no means unconscious, the child defeats the father by incorporating a part of the mother from which he can be reborn into an imaginary world transformed by fire. By accepting the feminine influence of reverie (in Jung, the vessel or container often symbolizes the feminine) and childhood, the Captain transforms the performance principle as well. Even when the Captain comes to equate his act with that of a caveman a million years ago discovering fire caused by lightning on a lonely northern trail—in a passage that, because of its confrontation of time scales is more an attempt at scientific validation than reverie—the caveman and his nervously smiling people find a kind of sensuous enjoyment in the gift of "summer" which comes before the interdiction of the Prometheus complex.

In Bradbury's imagination the advent of culture did not initially prevent the beginning of reverie. For the dreaming child, culture would be the extension of a natural reverie, and that is clearly what it becomes for the Captain here. As the Captain thinks of the new season in their cave, he offers us an image of fire, that newly acquired cultural object, that is almost a flower: ". . . this small yellow spot of changing weather" (p. 167). Now, a million years later, the Captain recapitulates that early gesture by which man transformed the potentialities of nature and himself. All of humanity is invited to participate:

> It took all of four seconds for the huge hand to push the empty Cup to the fire. So here we are again, today, on another trail, he thought, reaching for a cup of precious gas and vacuum, a handful of different fire with which to run back up cold space, lighting our way, and take to Earth a gift of fire that might burn forever. Why?
>
> He knew the answer before the question.
>
> Because the atoms we work with our hands, on Earth, are pitiful; the atomic bomb is pitiful and small and our knowledge is pitiful and small, and only the sun really knows what we want to know, and only the sun has the secret. And besides, it's fun, it's a chance, it's a great thing coming here, playing tag, hitting and running. There is no reason, really, except the pride and vanity of little insect men hoping to sting the lion and escape the maw. My God, we'll say, we *did* it! And here is our cup of energy, fire, vibration, call it what you will, that may well power our cities and sail our ships and light our libraries and tan our children and bake our daily breads and simmer the knowledge of our universe for us for a thousand years until it is well done. Here from this cup, all good men of science and religion: drink! Warm yourselves against the night of ignorance, the long snows of superstition, the cold winds of disbelief, and from the great fear of darkness in each man. So: we stretch out our hand with the beggar's cup. . . (p. 168)

One cannot stress too much the generosity of this passage. As the Captain touches the fire, he envisions a kind of ultimate cultural sublimation taking place upon their return to Earth. There is no indication that the sun's secret will destroy us—or the atom bomb, which appears "pitiful and small" (the atoms of which can be worked with the hand; again, the material imagination is active here) from the perspective of mankind's mature historical development through the conquest of space. Indeed, the Prometheus complex has itself been destroyed; no longer will it block the path to reverie and aesthetic sensuousness. Further, the reason for this mission is given as lying outside the sphere of knowledge to be gained by repression (scientific knowledge which, Bachelard has so ably demonstrated, proceeds by the repression of reverie). It is given as dominated by the play impulse, for the game itself. And the Captain knew the answer to this question before it was even asked, indicating to the reader who has been involved in this game that the reasons are not entirely hermeneutic ones.

When the problems of productivity have been mastered, Marcuse asserted, work is replaced by play, the performance principle by display. If we consider the number of flower images offered to us throughout this text (there are more to examine in a moment), we would seem to have a confirmation or validation of Marcuse's ideas. The Captain would offer his Cup, which is also a flower, for us to drink from. But what about the dialectical transformation of reason and sensuousness, are they part of the Captain's fantasy? Indeed, they seem to be. The Captain's reverie preserves the fantasy images of utopia: the energy of the sun will power and beautify our cities, light our libraries with knowledge, bake our daily bread (eliminate scarcity), tan our children (transform the body into aesthetic sensuousness based on leisure and play), simmer more knowledge of the universe for us (this time, gained without repression); nor will science and religion be any longer opposed. The sun's energy will cure both this century's disbelief and vanquish superstition and ignorance. As in true SF according to Suvin, Bradbury sees man's transformation as taking place within the horizon of science. He affirms that the space age offers us a chance to build the vision of paradise we have promised ourselves up until now only in our fantasies and religions (fantasy is clearly not a disparaging word to Bradbury, so I am not afraid to link his view of religion to it, and as he seems to do for the reader). Science and religion are ultimately concerned with the same thing, which the reader senses as belonging to *this* world and not to some occult logic of the supernatural, namely, gratification in free play of the released potentialities of man and nature.

Cooling, its heart pulse slowing, the ship turns away from the fire of the sun, while "the thermometer voice chanted the change of the seasons" (p. 168). If we have followed the oneiric level of meaning in this text closely, we might expect the text to break into poetry, to compose with images that sing reality and reveal being, because reverie wants to use language as Orphic praise. As the crew thinks with mild insouciance about the ultimate dream of controlling the climates of the imagination ". . . they might even dismantle some refrigerators, let winter die" (p. 168), the Captain, tending now to Bretton's body, remembers a poem he had composed many years before. The crew is living through a dynamic inversion of major proportions. Normally, we speak of "letting the *fire* die," and the price of our mastery over fire is never letting it go out. It involves us in a vigilance that requires the continual rennunciation of instinct. Now, however, it is possible to let winter's slumbering power die. What an inversion of the renunciation of instinct, won through reverie!

The Captain's poem celebrates and commemorates the new reality, pinpointing the general significance of the events he has lived through. The Captain's voice no longer commands, but sings of the labor of conquest, now over, and of the need to integrate the world of mythical childhood and peace with the adult world of death and loss:

> Sometimes I see the sun a burning Tree,
> Its golden fruit swung bright in airless air,
> Its apples wormed with man and gravity,
> Their worship breathing from them everywhere,
> As man sees Sun as burning Tree. . .

There are many echoes in this Orphic poem which mingles lyric religiosity and humanism. The poem is Orphic because it celebrates and upholds the golden fruit of being that is the beauty of this new world, now that they have the sun within them. Bradbury clearly recognizes the themes of lost infancy (Freud), the classical myth of the Hesperides, the blessed isles, and, of course, Yeats's famous poem of the wandering Aengus in quest of an imaginary world. Yet he follows the Bachelardian ontology of childhood in centering this poem with the archetype of the cosmic tree bearing the World Fruits which solicit our reverie and invite our happiness.[20] We feel the loss of man's autochthony in this uprooting age of technology, but Bradbury shows us that it is at least sometimes possible to find an axis integrating earth and sky in reverie.

There is also a suggstion of the burning bush from which God speaks to Moses, indicating that the poet mediates between man and God, naming what is holy for his age and communicating it to his fellow man. Technology is the god of our age, and there is a hint of elegiac sadness linking us to the world because of this fact, for Bradbury finds the golden apples "wormed with man and gravity." Gravity is, after all, what holds the human spirit down. It is gravity which causes the icicle to fall from the rooftop, breaking the child's reverie. The child may even know this scientific theory and know as well that the sun breathes in airless air. Perhaps, as the existentialist Sartre affirms, nothingness lies coiled at the heart of (the golden apple of) being like a worm, and it is only by resolutely facing up to the encounter with death and nothingness that we become authentically human. Yet there is the human possibility also, the poet reminds us, of seeing the world transformd by the child's fabulous imagination. And in contrast to physical gravitation, the force of gravity named in the tree is that which upholds being, lends a weight, a gravity, to the adventure of being. It draws beings toward itself as a center (their worship breathing from them everywhere).

The story at this point seems to have used up much of its narrative suspense, but there is still the thought of a joyous homecoming to Earth as the principle of proximity to being itself. The boy with a handful of dandelions is perhaps the most poignant image of the story, a moment which unites past, present, and future:

> The captain sat for a long while by the body, feeling many separate things. I feel sad, he thought, and I feel good, and I feel like a boy coming home from school with a handful of dandelions. (p. 169)

The Captain, and we as readers, take again the path opened by the image towards a reverie of childhood and away from the Freudian instinctual dialectic of sadness and joy, Thanatos and Eros. The image appears as a third term mediating this alternating opposition. It is poignant because in it the Captain discovers the true source and value of what he has accomplished, despite its cost. The Promethean task, the cosmic gesture of stealing the sun's energy and binding or containing this potentially destructive force (which dwarfs the atom bomb) for the benefit of humanity, has awakened the wonder of potential childhood within him. Reason and technology have been used to transform society, but at the same time reason and wonder dialectically interpenetrate. On the oneiric level, the text searches for a childhood without complexes, lives through a series of inversions and negations. But we are given a transcendental vantage point from which to assess the significance of the events in the story. We learn that the child has his own imaginatively transformed cosmos. If there are scientific truths, then there are also oneiric truths which transform reality: even as we are crossing the cosmos we are crossing the summer fields of childhood, picking the sun's blissful flowers.

Bradbury as implied author structures a great deal of reverberation into this image. We find that it echoes variationally through the text at crucial oneiric moments—*Copa de Oro,* the oneiric goal of the text, which drips yellow flowers, and the prehistoric cultural taming of fire which presents us with the small yellow spot of changing weather. This image of repose, of tranquility and comfort of basking in the illumination of the sun's own flowers, liberates us from the responsibilities of the adult world of the performance principle. The Captain is finally at rest, having accomplished his dream. The little boy who has escaped from the schoolroom where culture complexes are learned and grafted onto an increasingly forbidden childhood has stolen the fire of the sun already. In dreaming on these flowers, we realize that the Captain must have dreamt his mission long before accomplishing it.

The image of the handful of flowers recapitulates the success of the mission, but it would be a mistake to think that images in this story simply echo the past. Because they are open and communicable acts of consciousness addressed to a core of childhood within us, their direction is also towards the future of readers to come. The little boy with a handful of flowers has a future direction, home: "When you've gone a long, long way down to the sun and touched it and lingered and jumped around and streaked away from it, where do you go then?" (p. 169). The crew does not respond, as it did at the beginning of the story, with a scientific attempt to validate their new situation. Their consciousness, together with ours as readers, has changed during this cosmic encounter. There is no problem with the communicability of the reverie; we have all experienced the same reverie which has been commemorated by a world-originating Orphic song. Their being will be expressed by the poetry of reverie:

> His men waited for him to say it out. They waited for him to gather all of the coolness and the whiteness and the welcom and refreshing climate of the word in his mind, and they saw him settle the word, like a bit of ice cream, in his mouth, rolling it gently.
>
> "There's only one direction in space from here on out," he said at last.
>
> They waited. They waited as the ship moved swiftly into cold darkness away from light.
>
> "North," murmured the captain. "North."
>
> And they all smiled, as if a wind had come up suddenly in the middle of a hot afternoon (p. 169).

At the rainbow's end of this story, the reader finds that the entire universe of the tale has been transformed, as well as the relationship of language and being. Language which was used pragmatically for commands and directions, now concentrates and reveals poetic being. Furthermore, the image has renewed language through an oneiric logic of invention that here seeks a kind of poetic closure. The image of cold in the Captain's mouth dynamically balances the image of hotness contained in the ship. It is an image of cold within warm, of words changing climate in the poet's warming breath. No longer is winter "ammoniated." Now it can be eaten without any care at all. In the original joys of childhood, says Bachelard, the word is edible, a utopian nourishment of our being. The word "North," however, provides directions for a new reverie based on a new relation to substance. The Captain and crew are going home wrapped in the special climate of childhood where words dream. The merest breath which once separated them from complete annihilation now sustains their being in the poet/Captain's words.

Does all this meet, I wonder, Suvin's requirements for valid SF? Probably not. Such arguments as I have made will not convince one as adamant as he about the need for stringent scientific validation of the reader's response in "true" SF.

Perhaps it is best to say in conclusion that "The Golden Apples of the Sun" is indeed a dream of power, but for all mankind. At the very least Bradbury has given us a fable of modern consciousness which often forgets, in its urge towards progress and technological innovation, its Promethean debt to the unconscious. Yet further: in the long story of mankind's quest for knowledge, he has transformed Prometheus into a child dreaming close to oneiric sources.

6

Reverie and the Utopian Novel

Although the utopian novel addresses itself to a reader, literary criticism has been primarily concerned with the author's point of view, paying little attention to how the reader might be affected. One notable exception to this rule is Richard Gerber's *Utopian Fantasy,* which brings out the important role of reader expectation in such works. In following the theme of the utopian traveller in the evolution of utopian fiction since the end of the nineteenth century, he notes that the general aesthetic problem of utopian literature—how to present us with a society already made—inevitably involves the reader in a search for the past history of the society, what he calls the "utopian past."

If the writer of utopia could express the ideas of his hypothetical model of society directly in the experience of his characters, Gerber explains, he could dispense with the argumentative essays—the exposition of utopian life and passages of undigested social theory that often mar the attempt to create an effective utopian novel. But in practice this is nearly impossible to avoid. The new world is simply too unfamiliar. And the creator of a fictional utopia has to present us with a new construct that must be explained to the reader much as the naturalist writer explained society to his readers, but without the initial familiarity of the latter's scenes.

For the nineteenth century, Gerber points to the example of William Morris's *News from Nowhere* as being typical of how the past is hardly ever made a dramatic problem. As in most utopian novels of this century, historical accounts or discussions of how the utopian society came to be are usually placed in a central part where a familiar repertoire of characters engage one another. Usually, the stranger or utopian wise man (Old Hammond in Morris's novel) meet and discuss all the important questions connected with the subject. Gerber argues that few utopian novels of this sort are successful at making the society come alive for the reader because of the reader's position in the historical account—he is being passively informed rather than actively searching for the meaning of the utopian past for himself. These discursive passages, Gerber concludes, inevitably slow down the pace of the reader's exploration and discovery so that the reader is barely made to feel what it would be like to live in such a utopia.

This last requirement Gerber takes to be the historical task of the utopian tradition and the uppermost desire of utopian authors throughout the historical period his book encompasses.

Gerber also observes what happens to the reader's role in twentieth century utopian fiction, where an assimilation of techniques from the modern novel enables utopian writers to effect their desire for a complete society on the reader with more direct means than didactic arguments and discussions. The imaginary journey with its functional type, the pseudo-naive traveller who reminds us of the unreality of the utopian world by his very presence in it, gives way to a new kind of plot which he terms "completely utopian action."[1] In this type of story (Gerber lists Orwell's *1984* and Huxley's *Brave New World* as examples) the historical account has been effectively absorbed into the structure of the novel. Interest centers in the utopian characters and their existential problems which are directly presented (we might say through the system of perspectives that Iser has outlined as the underlying structure of the novel). More importantly, the reader is acquainted with the utopian world by means of an initial shock or surprise (a defamiliarization, we might say) instead of a gradual transition. This surprise enables the utopian writer to attain the closest possible connection with the reader's present-day reality. The reader must of necessity try to familiarize himself with his estranged surroundings (by projecting images into the text). In this manner, and by individual strategies which we need not examine here, *1984* and *Brave New World* bring the reader to actively imagine the utopian society for himself: "At last the utopian writer's aim has been achieved: utopia has come alive, the reader becomes a citizen of the imaginary world."[2]

This traditional desire to achieve the effect of an imaginary society goes along with Gerber's system of aesthetic values in utopian fantasy. Gerber proposes a series of touchstones for the successful utopian novel which can easily be integrated into Iser's theory. Gerber says that in general the reader must feel the presence of a consistently worked-out fundamental hypothesis, first by giving it imaginative reality and then by following it through all its ramifications. Furthermore, the utopian novel must present us with a society worked out in *suggestive* detail. The narrative must work on the reader's imagination with more than just statistics, arguments, or discussions. If there is any satire implicit in the contrast of the two societies (the reader's and the one presented in the book,) it cannot be merely didactic: the reader must feel it for himself. Most importantly for Gerber, the novel's imaginary society should seem to be alive, and we should be made to feel what it would be like to live in such a utopia (utopia must be given full ontological status as an imaginative reality—not written off by the author as just a "fantasy" as W. R. Irwin's study would seem to indicate). And finally, Gerber's aesthetic value system requires that after reading a negative utopia (dystopia or anti-utopia) the reader should be thoroughly and experientially dissatisfied with the present state of society: he will have worked out for himself through the exercise of his own utopian imagination the meaning of the novel's latent social criticism.

Beyond this modicum of expectation, we should refrain at the outset from imposing any abstract generic schemes on our reading of *Fahrenheit 451,* for those critics who have not done so have been led by their preconceptions to derive false interpretations from a true response. A good case in point is John Huntington's recent study of utopian and anti-utopian logic in the novel. Huntington claims that the novel moves from dystopia to utopia, from negative to positive without evoking any critical positions in between, and he thinks that this is a deep structural contradiction which cannot be mediated except in a "blurred" fashion (imagery and evocation rather than true thought): "The dystopian and utopian possibilities in the novel are thus represented by separate clusters of images that the novel finds unambiguous and leaves unchallenged."[3] Indeed, in this view of the text, mediation produces horror rather than thought. Nature is good and technology is bad, but the ultimate horror is a mixture of the two, the mechanical hound, which combines the relentlessness of the bloodhound with the infallibility of technology.

But if both possibilities depend on systems of imagery that ignore contradictions, Huntington goes on to note the very presence of contradiction in the novel's central symbol:

> The interesting difficulty is where do books fit into this simple opposition? Since Gutenberg the book has been a symbol of technological progress. Bradbury counters this meaning of his symbol by reducing his pastoral, not to paper books, but to humans who remember books. Thus the replication and general availability that are books' virtues, but which the novel has seen as the instruments of the mass-culture that has ruined the world, are denied. We have the *idea* of the book without the *fact* of its production. Then, by becoming a general symbol of the past now denied, the book becomes a symbol for all old values, but this symbolism brings up two difficulties. First, whatever good books have propagated, they have also preached the evils that have oppressed the world. The very technology that the novel finds threatening would be impossible without books. Second, books can readily inspire a repressive and tradition-bound pedantry which, while anti-technological, is also against nature.[4]

One wonders how Huntington could have arrived at this awareness of contradictions if the novel in fact so studiously avoids them. Thus Huntington is confused by the end of the novel where he sees the moral vision of the novel and its ideal of radiant literacy made subject to a "titanic revision of values." But to read it this way would be to suppose that Bradbury is attempting anti-utopian thought, which he admits seems unlikely. These difficulties are the result of genre theory, narrowly conceived. If Huntington had remained true to his actual experience of reading, instead of trying to impose an abstract scheme on it, he would have been led to discover the complex dialectical process by which the social criticism of the novel is effected and to a clearer perception of its themes. On the oneiric level, mediations are everywhere suggested, and as we will show later they evoke anything but horror.

The reader's search for the meaning and significance of utopia is in essence the subject of the book, as should be obvious from the fact that the protagonist, Montag the fireman, is caught up as a reader himself in the very contradictions Huntington mentions. This is what makes the book's portrayed world so dramatic and easily realized (quite apart from the fact that fire itself easily and dramatically brings about the phenomena of a fantastic world). Its main hypothesis—that technology, mass culture, and minority pressure brought about the world we see portrayed in the novel—is indeed made concrete for the reader *because* of the very contradictions of books. I do not mean that *Fahrenheit 451* is contradictory in the sense that it refutes its own hypothesis, but only that it does not deny the negative and contradictory values of books themselves. Why this negative value needs to be preserved is something we can now elaborate on.

Fahrenheit 451 makes vivid for the reader the whole problematic course of Western enlightenment that culminated in technology and the positivistic processes of thought its world-wide dominance have brought about. In order to know nature objectively we in a sense misrecognize or forget ourselves as part of nature. The price of progress is brought about by a kind of oblivion, like that of a surgical operation on our bodies during which we were unconscious or anesthetized. Consciousness once more restored, we find it difficult to bridge the gap between our present and our past: "The loss of memory is a transcendental condition for science. All objectification is a forgetting."[5] The disenchantment of nature and myth brings about a certain triumph of man over his fears, but by defining man in opposition to nature it sets up a program for domination and so reverts to barbarism and mythic repetition. Thus like the phoenix symbol used in the novel, history in *Fahrenheit 451* appears to go in cycles. The irony seems to be that the capacity to know and represent the world to ourselves is the measure of our domination of it, but domination—power and knowledge—are the things most often represented. Language itself (as that of Fire Chief Beatty in the novel) is used deceitfully as a tool for domination: "The capacity of representation is the vehicle of progress and regression at the same time."[6]

It is understandable then that this dialectical process is represented in *Fahrenheit 451* as a fantastic reversal of the real world. Firemen who should control fires (perhaps the ultimate symbol of technology in the novel) are lighting them instead. The reader is at first surprised by this when the novel opens immediately with a scene of house burning or arson in which Montag takes pleasure in burning books, and it sets him off on his quest for understanding the relationship between this fantastic world and his own. It is also therefore a contradiction within the imagery system of the dystopian world itself, for how can the technological world be represented by natural imagery? It seems that we must find a non-alienating way to represent the demands of unrecognized nature. Fire in this world can only be ironic enlightenment.

The principles of this false enlightenment are made apparent to the reader by the book's vitriolic attack on mass culture, which turns out to be a permanent denial of pleasure despite the power it displays and promises. No modern utopian novel insists more than *Fahrenheit 451* on the nonidentity of culture and society. The book struggles at every point to double or split the reader's forced and false identification with the society which has nurtured him. It compels the reader to discover for himself the passivity of the subject in mass culture, his loss of critical autonomy and freedom, and the general decline of negative critical forces in society—forces which could lead to a critique of existing conditions if not to utopia. This splitting constantly happens to Montag in his readings and is dramatized especially in the second part of the novel. It is here that the book registers a deeply felt fear that mass culture is threatening to collapse art as an autonomous realm of utopian freedom into the mere mechanical reproduction and repetition of the economic base. Why are books banned in this society? The reader discovers with Montag that they are the only thing left which harbors the forces of negation or principles through which the world around us could be made to appear false and alienating (what the implied author obviously thinks is the case). As the utopian wise man Faber says, books show the pores in the face of life, its gaps and discontinuities.

But what role does reverie have in the novel? This only emerges clearly in the third part of the novel when Montag has escaped the city. The third part of Bradbury's hypothesis is realized here. It was minority pressure which combined with the other two forces which eventually led to the need for everyone to be the same—to narcissism, in short. People must be mirror images of each other which means that they never have any real contact with a world outside themselves. And advertising and other media techniques are bent on artificially stimulating the consumption of grandiose images of the self within the city itself. This psychological theme is very prominent in *Fahrenheit 451*, and it is surprising that no critic has made much of it since Kingsley Amis twenty years ago.

Amis argued that the lesson to be drawn from *Fahrenheit 451* is not only that a society could be devised that would frustrate active virtues, nor even that these could eventually be suppressed, but that there is in all kinds of people something that longs for this to happen. This need presupposes not some kind of overt political action (indeed, no violent military takeover or class struggle is indicated in the novel), but a tendency in human behavior that could be reinforced if certain tendencies presently at work in society were not corrected or mitigated. Analyzing a scene from *Fahrenheit 451* in which Mildred, Montag's wife, is near suicide from a drug overdose and is listening only to the noise of an electronic Seashell, he concludes that it demonstrates to him a "fear of pleasure so overmastering that it can break down the sense of reality or at least the pattern of active life, and break them down in everyone, not merely in the predisposed neurotic."[7] Now, it is the experience of reverie in the third part of the novel which connects us to a real natural world (an arcadian utopia, in fact) outside the narcissim of the city. The reader rediscovers through a long water-reverie, which is the exact opposite of Mildred's, the archetypes of utopian satisfaction. We experience with Montag a non-alienating relationship to nature, and this experience of the imaginary, of another world not based on domination, enables us to effect an oneiric criticism of technological society.

It is Bradbury's strategy to link initially the experience of reverie and world with Clarisse, Montag's teenage neighbor. Montag knows that all books that are works of art are connected with her in some way, for she awakens in him the desire to read (to create an imaginary world). But we must also be given some distance from this experience of the imaginary if we are to effect social criticism. To iden- tify completely with a character in a novel or play, as Madame Bovary and Don Quixote do, to become the book, is romantic madness and Faber tells Montag so in the book's central section. This sort of narcissism is resisted early in the book; the reader is repeatedly split, and we should therefore not be surprised at the end when Granger, the leader of the book people, tells Montag that he is not impor- tant, but the book he remembers is. Books must preserve their independent, autonomous and negative character, if they are to aid us in transforming basic im- pulses in the personality such as narcissism. Works of art, therefore, by represen- ting deprivation as negative retract, as it were, the prostitution of the utopian im- pulse by the culture industry and rescue by mediation what was denied: "The secret of aesthetic sublimation is its representation of fulfillment as a broken promise. The culture industry does not sublimate; it represses."[8] In Bradbury's novel media are not mediations unless they have some historical content to transform in the first place. Books are the repositories of that content, the novel's utopian past.

So Bradbury's novel is itself negative in representing utopia as a broken promise and pessimistic to the extent that utopian alternatives seem to be pre- served nowhere else than in the damaged lives of cultural outsiders. Yet it must be that Bradbury believes that social freedom is inseparable from enlightened thought, from remembering the mistakes of the past and not from forgetting them, because he holds out the promise that after this new Dark Age man may begin again. At the end of *Fahrenheit 451* books are no longer symbols of techno- logical progress—of power and knowledge—but rather of wisdom.

Roughly, that is the course of the reader's discovery in the novel. It remains to be shown in detail how the reader builds up an understanding of these themes by means of a repertoire of patterns serving an overall strategy through which the world of *Fahrenheit 451* is presented. As previously mentioned, there are two op- posed imagery systems in the novel. They have been isolated and independently studied by thematic criticism, as has the elaborate system of allusions and quota- tions in the novel.[9] They are in fact two different modes of fantasy, one leading to existential and reflexive use of the imagination in which the self can represent a world to itself in a non-alienated fashion, the other undermining the self's ability to conceive of anything outside of a fragmented dream. Together they constitute the poles of the suspended system of equivalences that the reader activates in reading the novel, which unfolds in a dialectical three-part structure as I have indicated.

In a first reading, and not by reading selectively to illustrate the imaginative and moral values of the novel, as we will do in a moment, the reader of *Fahrenheit 451* is immediately struck by the fact that the implied author has chosen to select and "depragmatize" a certain mode of fantasy as representing the dominant ideological systems of the fifties. Why, the reader asks, has this one been chosen and not another? Specifically, why is Montag's job (which is supposedly so important to the maintenance of order) treated as a carnival, and why is he a kind of clown? Why is happiness and not freedom the ideal of this society?

This simultaneous evocation and depragmatization of images representing the "culture industry" (*Kulturindustrie*—the term is Theodor Adorno's) leads the reader to project acts of consciousness into the text under conditions very different from that in which he experiences these media in real life. The reader thereby discovers deficiencies or contradictions inherent in such a system. The selection and intensification of Freudian fantasy (perhaps best exemplified by his book *The Interpretation of Dreams*, which discusses the unconscious processes involved in the dream's staging and representation of fulfilled desire) by the repertoire brings the reader to discover a destructive core of narcissism pervading the world of the novel, and by direct implication, the society around him.

I find that Christopher Lasch's *The Culture of Narcissism* (1979) simplifies but still gets at the essential criticism that Bradbury's reader has to enact. Lasch's point is that people in the "society of the spectacle" (and by that he means the specific social and economic environment of the post-World War II period) have lost the experience of real satisfaction because of the fabrication of so many pseudo-needs by industrial civilization. Uninterrupted advertising transmitted by mass media uses Freudian images of utopian satisfaction not so much to create desire (which in Freud's system is related to a lost object anyway) as to activate anxiety about one's self-image.[10] Indeed, the similarities are so striking in so many details that I am tempted to agree with French post-structuralist thinkers such as Louis Marin who argue that at a determined moment of history, utopian textual practice sketches or schematizes unconsciously, by the spatial plays of its internal differences (non-congruences), the empty places (topics) which will be filled by the concepts of social theory in a later phase of history.[11] To write a utopia is to *indicate* what cannot yet be *said* within the available language.

But this would be to deconstruct my own phenomenological project, perhaps the subject for a future book, but hardly compatible with my view here of the temporal unfolding of meaning for the reader of *Fahrenheit 451*, which, as in all fantasy based on reverie, exists in a realm between the unspeakable and the conceptually spoken, the realm of the poetic word. It would also be to deny that the utopian novel can effect critical thought in the reader, is more than a "neutral-ization" of society's contradictions. For the moment it is best to bracket the rela-tionship between social theory and literature, although Bradbury's book did appear at a time when many studies purported to analyse the psychological im-pact of social changes on character structure: Eric Fromm's "market-oriented personality," or William H. Whyte's famous "organization man" being two ob-vious examples. It may be, as Lasch says, that these social theorists mistook the bland surface of American sociability for the deeper reality, which he believes was the creation of a narcissistic personality amenable to social domination, but such arguments, interesting as they are in themselves, would take us too far afield.

In any case Bradbury does lay bare the hidden violence and emptiness of this sort of personality. The reader cannot organize the image-sequences of the pro-grammed fantastic (or so I term the fantasy of the telescreens) which represents the world of appearances, into a coherent experience. Furthermore, we are made aware by a constant ironic switching of character perspectives that the self-mastery and happiness preached by the advocates of this mode of fantasy is com-pletely false. Their inner selves are exposed as chaotic and impulse-ridden. Both Fire Chief Beatty and Mildred are deeply suicidal.

Once the reader discovers that Freudian fantasy has been selected to per-sonify negative trends in our society (especially advertising and debased romantic fantasies, "the Clara Dove five-minute romance"), he is also led, through the ac-tivation of his own archetypal imagination in reverie, to seek out and consider solutions to the problems raised by the programmed fantastic. This is tied together with Montag's search for the utopian past, as I have mentioned, and his readings produce a system of allusions and quotations which guide us in this proc-ess by stimulating, however briefly, the experience of the imaginary, the promise of a world of meaning that can only be given through literature. Thus both modes of fantasy converge on the problem of utopia through a process of coherent deformation, a reciprocal projection and contrast of images drawn from both systems.

The search for answers to the utopian past is, as Gerber indicates, an aspect of plot which needs to be integrated into the experience of the main character. *Fahrenheit 451* accomplishes this through its strategies. In particular, the ex-perience of literacy as a new psychic faculty is organized by a theme-and-horizon strategy which now foregrounds and now allows to be part of the background the reading of forbidden books. This strategy controls the dialectical contradictions experienced by Montag, who goes from being a burner of books curious about what they contain, to a Promethean reader who wants to redeem all culture, to a chastened man who assumes responsibility for his existence, and, by resolutely committing himself to memorize a part of the Bible, for the healing of others. The plot of *Fahrenheit 451,* if we wanted to discuss it apart from the demands of signification made on the reader, is not simply an inversion from positive to negative or vice-versa. The mediations go from ignorance to knowledge and from knowledge to its enunciation as the novel ends.

Despite the apparent oppositional arrangement of the repertoire, which would seem to require that the text set norms against one another by showing up the deficiencies of each norm when viewed from the standpoint of the others, in a process of reciprocal negation and continual conflict, in actuality the strategy embodied in *Fahrenheit 451* is much simpler, closer to what Iser terms the counterbalancing arrangement, and to the traditional utopian novel.[12] In this arrangement the elements of the repertoire allotted to different perspectives form a very definite hierarchy. Qualities and defects of the perspectives are clearly graded. The hero represents the principal perspective through which a catalogue of norms is unfolded. In *Fahrenheit 451* Montag is intended to be an effective counterbalancing visualization of that which the society of spectacles seems to exclude — an exemplary concern for the rights of others and a world outside the self. Nevertheless, the norms of the culture industry take place in a context of negated and negating perspectives—a context quite different from the system out of which they were selected. This is tantamount to saying that the reader becomes aware of the influences and functions they perform in real life. And Clarisse, a minor character by objective standards because she disappears early in the novel, is in essence the inspirational anima figure of Montag's quest. She represents those imaginative values he lacks and which he must acquire. Otherwise the social norms and imaginative values of the repertoire are assigned to perspectives that are subtly undermined. Those characters attracted to fantasy-spectacle (Mildred and Fire Chief Beatty) have complexes which reveal a hidden ontological insecurity which they have not consciously faced. Even Faber's ideal of radiant literacy is undercut, but self-consciously by himself.

What this amounts to saying is that the reader must pay special attention to the oneiric level of the text, the transcendental vantage point which eventually he must build up in order to have a coherent aesthetic response to the text's world and from which the events and characters are to be imagined. Nowhere is this more necessary than in the case of the mechanical hound and the sense of uneasiness it is intended to provoke. This feeling of uneasiness or uncanniness is linked to the oneiric strategy of making the reader become aware of the nonidentity of society and culture. The reader must be doubled or made self-conscious of it. Treated objectively (as Huntington and W. R. Irwin seem to do) the hound represents another character perspective, a failed mediation, or the dragon on Montag's quest. On the oneiric level of significance, however, it is the embodiment of the uncanny return of our existential problems that we have attempted to banish with the use of technology. It represents also the history of repressed nature which follows its own underground logic: "It was like a bee come home from some field where the honey is full of poison wildness, of insanity and nightmare, its body crammed with that overrich nectar..."[13]

Huntington says that mediation in this novel produces only horror, which is a true response on the affective level, but it is also a contradiction or negation or mediation because the reader wants to know why technology is represented by alienated natural imagery. Interpreted in a dialectical-historical fashion, these images yield up their truth and cognitive value: this is not the utopian nectar of the gods on Olympus, offering eternal bliss, but that of some dark underworld; it is surely not wisdom or spiritual riches either, but the representation of the productivity and abundance of nature gone awry. What is "that overrich nectar"? The obedient activity of dominated nature, the bee, produces only poison for us by some process that is now mysterious. Like a nightmare it seems alien to conscious life, and cannot be integrated into it. Yet the bee has come home to its hive, our society, and is fimiliar to us. The material imagination aids us in understanding the oneiric level of significance here, which is much more than metaphor, and in transforming historical content. Thus the reader's response has to be both cognitive and sublimative; he is doubled or split by the initial uncanniness, but in responding he must make full use of his humanity.

W. R. Irwin's response to the novel is interesting in this regard, for he reports that the mechanical hound evokes no uneasiness in him and that the reader is not doubled. Irwin's rhetoric of fantasy, *The Game of the Impossible*, argues that the reader's role in any fantasy text is a kind of "dual participation" because fantasy is a demonstrational narrative dominated by intellectual persuasion. The reader is persuaded by the author's rhetoric to accept an "anti-fact" which is then developed by intellectual play. But the reader must be kept continuously aware that he is engaged with the impossible as a factitious reality—there can be no surprises or ambiguities about the rules of the game of the impossible (Irwin's theory is in fact the exact logical opposite of Todorov's). The reader "must feel at all times intellectually 'at home' in the narrative and yet maintain his sense of intellectual alienation as a means of reflecting on the displaced real."[14] According to Irwin, *Fahrenheit 451* is not a fantasy because its narrative does not deal with the impossible and does not evince utopian thinking that asserts and plays with the idea of an impossible society. Incredibly, Irwin bases these conclusions not on an analysis of the reader's role in *Fahrenheit 451*, or even on a consideration of what the generic role of the reader is in utopian fantasy, but on the supposed science-fiction *content* of the novel. Science fiction, he says, while it may deal with the improbable, does not assert "the thing which is not."[15] After summarizing the plot of the novel he goes on to affirm:

> My point is that all the devices by which tyranny is secured either exist at present or may be foreseen as probable technological developments of the near future. Even the Mechanical Hound puts no strain on belief; it is a not very daring instance of the malevolent robot. And we are all used to robots. I feel safe in saying that no machine that possesses super-animal or superhuman capabilities can prompt a reader to say "impossible."[16]

Quite apart from the fact that this analysis cannot be made to agree with Irwin's own normative statement that "to define a genre by its material content alone is a mistake,"[17] one senses in the background and from his disparagement of reverie in general the presence of a non-dialectical Aristotelian logic with its categories of probable, improbable and impossible. This sort of logic cannot deal with dialectical contradiction or the Freudian logic of the uncanny. Irwin reports that he "feels safe" in his response to the mechanical hound, but also that the narrative did not make him feel at home while engaging in a game of contradictory credences (in other words, this is science fiction, not fantasy; but we are all familiar with robots). Again one wonders whether a true response has been falsified by the imposition of a foreign logical scheme. The recognition that we are the source of strangeness, and that we cannot escape our existential problems by the use of technology and representational logic, constitutes an uncanny feeling to say the least.

In what follows I shall be concerned only to point out instances of the reader's developing response to the oneiric level of the text. Limitations of space forbid my giving a narrative reading as in previous chapters.

In part I, "The Hearth and the Salamander," the main events are the opening scene of arson, already mentioned, Montag's meeting with Clarisse, Mildred's attempted suicide, our first encounter with the mechanical hound, another fire in which an old woman chooses to die with her books (and during which Montag steals a volume), Clarisse's disappearance, Montag's subsequent illness or alienation from his work, and Beatty's attempt to win him back through a defense of utopia. It ends with Montag's decision to find out for himself whether books contain anything worth dying for.

How are these events and characters to be imagined? To begin with, the title of this section is clearly ironic, for houses in this future society have all been "fire proofed." There is no possibility for a fireside reverie in which man might find repose in centering his consciousness on a specific object. The landscape is instead infested with a cold mythical beast, the fire engine/Salamander that "spits its venomous kerosene upon the world"(p. 3). Montag is also a part of this landscape, and his complex emerges in the following lines: "...his hands were the hands of some amazing conductor playing all the symphonies of blazing and burning to bring down the tatters and charcoal ruins of history" (p.3) One critic has called it a "Nero complex" and I see no reason to change this designation.[18] Besides, it provides a useful semantic index for the reader in later contexts where the complex is being transformed. In the second part, where Montag learns from Faber that books are a counter force to man's narcissism, he is told that books exist to remind us" '...what asses and fools we are. They're Caesar's praetorian guard, whispering as the parade roars down the avenue, "Remember, Caesar, thou art mortal' " (p.93). And in the third part, Granger further tells Montag to forget security, to see the world outside himself that is more fantastic than any dream made or paid for in the factories of the culture industry, to hate the Roman named Status Quo (p. 170).

The first step towards the transformation of this complex is Montag's meeting with Clarisse on a moonlit sidewalk on his way home from work. Ostensibly happy and adjusted to his work and society, a minstrel man, Montag is gently divided against himself during their encounter:

> He saw himself in her eyes, suspended in two shining drops of bright water, himself dark and tiny, in fine detail, the lines about his mouth, everything there, as if her eyes were two miraculous bits of violet amber that might capture and hold him intact. Her face, turned to him now, was fragile milk crystal with a soft and constant light in it. It was not the hysterical light of electricity but—what? But the strangely comfortable and rare and gently flattering light of the candle. One time, as a child, in a power-failure, his mother had found and lit a last candle and there had been a brief hour of rediscovery, of such illumination that space lost its vast dimensions and drew comfortably around them, and they, mother and son alone, transformed, hoping that the power might not come on again too soon . . . (pp. 7-8)

Himself reflected in miniscule in the miraculous water of Clarisse's eyes, in fine aesthetic detail, Montag is given a tranquil affirmation of his being. The material imagination is present here in amber, the scented hardened fossil resin "wept" from trees. This substance is naturally miraculous because it preserves fossils and time. Montag can see himself in the heart of matter, transparent, intact, and living (unlike the melted tallow skin of his false face which comes later). The amber is oneirically appropriate for Clarisse (and her object reveries), expressing her love and knowledge of the natural world and the past. But more significantly, a world of intersubjectivity is granted here: in the instantaneous moment of the image, which usually inaugurates reverie, Montag rediscovers a dimension of consciousness lost to this society which paradoxically is saturated with image-spectacles (so much so that he wears a fiery permanent smile on his face, as if he were being recorded and simultaneously transmitted to an unseen audience—another aspect of narcissism). On the level of reflexive reading indicated here, this passage shows us what a reverie text can do, namely, mirror the process of intersubjectivity in reading, of that moment when we feel another consciousness enclosing ours.

Furthermore, this reassuring act of consciousness is tied to our experience of childhood in subtle ways. Husserl, the founder of phenomenology as the eidetic science of the possible structures of consciousness, argued that the first formal act (*der erste Aktus*) that constitutes the child *as* child is an act of empathy stemming from the felt awareness of the other (usually the mother's face or glance) and the subsequent communicating and working with the other. Husserl suggests that through the act of empathy the child comes to see itself as appearing for the other, in the other's surrounding world, and, at the same time, the child comes to see the other as appearing for the child, in the child's life-world. For Husserl, the mirroring structure of the glance is founded on the recognition of the other as an enti-ty existing independently of the child, though supporting him. It is an act of consciousness that opens also new possibilities of love and empathic being, possi-bilities of transcendence towards a common horizon, instead of the infinite repetition of the same. Such phenomenological interrelatedness gives rise, he says, "to an infinite reciprocal 'mirroring' . . . an unlimited reiteration which is a potentiality for levels of empathy."[19] Thus Montag is brought back to his child-hood and the security of reverie in a single instant.

This movement of consciousness is clarified and developed when Montag searches for an equivalent to the soft constant light of Clarisse's face and discovers the memory of a utopian past in a reverie towards childhood that is the opposite of the fantasy world of the programmed fantastic (here represented by the hysterical light of electricity). The light of her face is not the hysterical light of electricity, but the generic light of *the* candle, the light of reverie texts, a human-ized light lacking in this technologically oriented society. That light which is strangely comfortable and gently flattering (already the candle speaks poetically and we can imagine an admiring glance between self and world) assures the reader that he is going to discover in this passage the shadings of an ontology of well-being, or reverie. The candlelight which gathers dispersed being around the dreamer awakens the reflexive dimension of consciousness lost to this society: reading.

By leaving the end of his last sentence blank and in suspension, "hoping that the power might not come on again too soon . . . ," Bradbury structures a gap which the reader has to fill in with his own imagination of what the mother and son *did* after they lit the candle and space lost its vast dimensions, drawing com-fortably around them in humanized reverie. In that brief hour of rediscovery where the mother and son are transformed, I imagine they are reading, perhaps even a book of fairy tales. And as Bachelard indicates in a book devoted entirely to a philosophic meditation on reveries of the candle flame, the lifting force of this vertical-tending reverie is the most liberating of all, especially when it dreams of another possible world above the prosaically horizontal, or in the case of the pro-grammed fantastic, circular, life.[20] In oneiric terms, the candle flame is both strange and comfortable because it allows for shadows (indeed, shadows seem part of its valiant struggle to be) and for the unconscious mind under the bene-ficial influence of the anima to make the candle flame's struggle for illumination and its frail vertical existence into our own because of our own desire for transcendence. The flames of hell are certainly transforming, but they belong properly to the fantastic, not to the delicate penumbral ontology of Bachelardian reverie where the values of the dream and reality can be freely explored.

So the oneiric level of significance discovered by Montag in his reverie of the candle's flame is very much the opposite of the on/off logic of the light switch which controls the source of illumination in these "fire-proofed" houses. Our only role in technological illumination is to be the mechanical subject of a mechanical gesture. "We have entered in the era of administered light," Bachelard says of our loss of the ability to make the light of candles and lamps our own through reverie, humanizing the world and making ourselves at home in it.[21] Bradbury would seem to agree, for mother and son are very much at home in the solitude of the candle flame. Having gathered our reverie of verticality around us, and having glimpsed with Montag the possibility of transcendence of his situation, we can well understand their hopeful consciousness that the lights will not come on again too soon and destroy the beneficial influence of reading in anima.

If I seem to stress Clarisse unduly, it is because her perspective is held up as one of the ideals of the novel, at least initially. Her reveries in which consciousness intimately touches the reality of the material universe offset the erosion of Montag's capacity to dream. Through his encounters and talks with her he rediscovers the power of reading in anima (and later, when he begins to read more resolutely, he realizes that "These men have been dead a long time, but I know their words point, one way or another, to Clarisse." (p.78). Although she is presumed dead early in the novel, her spirit returns in the third section when Montag is finally able to represent a utopian experience to himself.

A gentle hunger and curiosity, a desire to look at things as epiphanies of a marvelous reality, pervades the presence in the novel of this anima figure. Obviously she has a very deep sympathy with nature. When Montag first meets her out walking one enchanted moonlit night, the leaves and the wind seem to carry her forward like a wood spirit along the sidewalk (p. 5). Her unique slender face is wholly outward-looking, nourishing itself on things. Furthermore she constantly probes Montag's identification with his job by asking him questions ("Do you ever *read* any of the books you burn?" (p. 8), shocks him with her knowledge of the past (firemen once put out fires instead of lighting them) and of the present (how advertising billboards have been made two hundred feet long so that speeding drivers can read them, whereas grass is a green blur, cows are brown blurs). She lives surrounded by a loving family in a house brightly lit at night where Montag can hear human conversation weaving its magic spell (p. 18).

Bachelard tells us that the subject in reverie is astonished to receive the image, astonished and awakened. When Montag's capacity for reverie is awakened, it is always Clarisse's face (her very name is a simulacrum of reflected light) that will guide him: "The girl's face was there, really quite beautiful in memory: astonishing, in fact" (p. 11). But her own reveries are object reveries, a simple faithfulness to the familiar object. Bachelard says that in object reveries we learn to dream near things and explore our attachment to the world. Clarisse tries to stimulate these reveries in Montag. She leaves a bouquet of late autumn flowers on his porch, or a handful of chestnuts in a little sack or some autumn leaves neatly pinned to a sheet of white paper and thumbtacked to his door. Although her reveries are not the complexly layered structures of consciousness that Montag will develop in his long water reverie, she can do things with a common dandelion flower that reveal Montag's inner being. Her consciousness is infused with objects of the world: there seems to be no distance between them and her, so faithful and welcoming is her glance. Clarisse is truly one of Bachelard's dreamers of looking (*rêveurs du regard*) who can raise objects to a level of poetic existence, and therefore of human existence.[22]

In addition to awakening wonder in the contemplation of the ordinary itself (we are told her face is "fragile milk-crystal," a seemingly commonplace object but evoking at the same time a recognition of it as an exceptional phenomenon, a cool stillness in a world of fiery conflagrations) Clarisse does three things for Montag. First of all, Montag receives from her gaze not a narcissistic mirror image, but a tranquil affirmation of his existence, which is also an act of empathy and a genuine intersubjective relation with an other. Second, she awakens in him an other experience of temporality, an ontological sensitization to the future. The girl's simple wonder at the things of this world (her pale surprise, the narrator says) make her fore-sighted in a utopian sense.[23] Third, she contributes to the level of reflexive reading in the text by stimulating Montag's reading in anima. The second and perhaps most utopian of these accomplishments emerges in the following passage, where the narrative mode creates the effect of a strange mental process (reverie) suddenly intruding into Montag's mind:

> Montag shook his head. He looked at a blank wall. The girl's face was there, really quite beautiful in memory: astonishing in fact. She had a very thin face like the dial of a small clock seen faintly in a dark room in the middle of the night when you waken to see the time and see the clock telling you the hour and the minute and the second, with a white silence and a glowing, all certainty and knowing what it has to tell of the night passing swiftly on toward further darknesses, but moving also toward a new sun.
>
> "*What?*" asked Montag of that other self, the subconscious idiot that ran babbling at times, quite independent of will, habit, and conscience. (p. 11)

Here we can observe a penumbral reverie forming in Montag's mind, beginning with the astonishment of the image (the girl's face in memory), then moving on to a search for an equivalent to that astonishment, a clock seen in the middle of the night upon awakening, and then onward to a sequence where technological segments of time (hours, minutes, seconds) are more and more minutely divided, until only a durational flow, a continuous pulse of experiential time, remains. Montag awakens to discover a new consciousness of time as sustaining the forms of life instead of destroying them. The clock's face is a white silence and a glowing. Like the moon in Montag's long water reverie in the novel's concluding section, it shines by reflected light, not burning time, but telling us where we are. Compensating Montag for a lack in his conscious mind, Clarisse enables him to project unconscious feminine values. An image received from the anima puts Montag's mind in a state of continuous reverie; it is a time fully experienced and filled, disclosing to Montag an inexhaustible reserve of latent life. As Bachelard says, the clock of the feminine runs continuously in a duration that slips peacefully away, but the masculine clock is composed of technological segments, jerks of time, so many projects and ways of not being present to oneself.

One has the sense here also of being guided by the anima figure, because the feminine clock is certain of what it tells Montag: the darkness of the night will get darker, but there is no need for despair; we are also moving toward a new sun. We feel reassured in this strange new experience of time. Montag's reverie begins in memory (perhaps a memory of childhood, of awakening from a nightmare), but opens up to the future, toward not-yet-being, a pattern of consciousness which splits Montag from his identification with his social mask or persona. It lays down the temporal pattern of Montag's utopian longings.

On the oneiric level, meaning is constituted here by Montag's questioning *"'What'?"* directed towards that "other self," the archetypal shadow, which he has taken previously to be a fool but which he will want to educate through reading. Prior to this scene, Clarisse and Montag walk together for perhaps five minutes of objective clock time, yet now that time seems immense and numinous to him. The narrator says that her slender figure throws an "immense shadow" on the stage of his imagination. Indeed, it is clear that she reveals to him *his* shadow, without which he would be a one-dimensional man, his shadow which represents the large undiscovered part of himself that this society has repressed and excluded. In the Jungian development of individuation, the persona is the counterpart to the shadow, and its original existence is prompted to a large extent by the need to repress material inconsistent with the social environment. Until he meets Clarisse, Montag's ego is largely fused with his persona as a fireman, but the anima intervenes between these two figures and allows him to deal with his shadow in a manageable and integrative way, although not without a certain amount of anguish when the desire for illumination, expressed as a candle flame, becomes opaque and consciousness thickens into the substance of unhappiness:

> He felt his smile slide away, melt, fold over and down on itself like a tallow skin, like the stuff of a fantastic candle burning too long and now collapsing and now blown out. Darkness. He was not happy. He said the words to himself. He recognized this as the true state of affairs. He wore his happiness like a mask and the girl had run off across the lawn with the mask and there was no way of going to knock on her door and ask for it back. (p.12)

Here Montag is beginning to make the transition from identification with society to open rebellion against it. His unhappiness is further deepened by his discovery of Mildred's attempted suicide. She is Clarisse's opposite, a true victim of consumer culture. Inwardly, she is a frightened child in despair about ever knowing reality. Outwardly, however, she is an advertising man's dream, addicted to novelty, gadgets, and anxiety-easing pills, Her hair is burnt by chemicals to a brittle straw, her body thin as a praying mantis from dieting. Montag's relationship to her is always "mediated" by some desiring-machine of the media. At night she lies in bed with the little Seashells (remember Johnny Bishop, our other dreamer of the sea, and how he escaped the adult world?) or thimble radios, tamped tight in her ears, "and an electronic ocean of sound, of music and talk and music and talk coming in, coming in on the shore of her unsleeping mind" (p. 13). This is hardly a natural reverie of sea, since it is programmed by the media, and the fact that it is so unsatisfying is indicated by the fact that Mildred is unsleeping and suicidal: "There had been no night in the last two years that Mildred had not swum that sea, had not gladly gone down in it for the third time" (p. 13). Mildred is an expert at lip reading (ten years of study in this technique having been provided by the Seashell corporation) and when she has the Seashells in her ears, conversation is reduced to a kind of pantomime. The only thing Mildred seems to desire is the fourth parlor wall "to make the dream complete" (p. 22). If they had a fourth wall, she argues, then the room wouldn't be theirs anymore, but would belong to "all kinds of exotic people" (p. 22).

As Lasch has indicated, this is the pattern of pathological narcissism that advertising and consumer culture have reinforced through stimulating the desire to consume grandiose images of the self. Mildred's intrapsychic world is so thinly populated, consisting of these shadowy and specular images, that Montag in a moment of oneiric insight (derived, it is clear, from his dialogues with Clarisse,) senses the effect on Mildred's inner world of these mindless conversations emanating from the fantasy people who inhabit the T.V. walls (p. 47). Mildred is the little girl of a fairy tale, lost, however, without the hope traditionally granted to heroines by the spirit-figures of this genre which Jung has identified (the anima herself, the wise old man, the archetype of the tree of life which Montag rediscovers at the novel's end).[24] Mildred cannot find a way out of this insane asylum where the walls are always talking to her (where she is always talking to herself). Images of a real family have disappeared; fake images have taken their place. None of these "relatives" of the telescreen family will tell her a fairy tale, that traditional source of popular wisdom which, as Bettelheim indicates, offers a convincing view of the adult world to the child and which therefore builds a bridge to that world.[25] And if fairy tales are the oldest form of utopian narrative, as Ernst Bloch suggests, then there is something sadly lacking in this "utopia" which feels it must burn those allegedly terrifying stories.[26] The psychologistic age depicted in *Fahrenheit 451* has destroyed one of the primary means for assuring continuity of generations (since the child can come to feel, according to Bettelheim, that his parents do not inhabit a world that is totally alien to his own) and the memory of happy experiences. Recently, Ursula LeGuin has also written about the beneficial effects of these Jungian figures in fantasy and science fiction.[27]

What this amounts to is that Mildred has no culture complex outside of a very primitive narcissism. Society has provided her with no means, however contradictory, to transform her inner psychic world, which is seen even more clearly from the narrator's perspective during her attempted suicide. In a cleverly staged scene in which two impersonal "operators" come to the rescue with a kind of vacuum cleaner mounted with an electronic eye, we are made acutely aware of the individual's dependence on a bureaucratized state and the "helping professions," those outside experts who intervene in family problems. The irony of the scene is that they are not even doctors, but "handymen," since suicide has become so common that it required the production of a new machine to deal specifically with the problem, and with a new job speciality. At the same time as we are working out for ourselves the depths of irony in which no one is really getting at the real problems behind Mildred's suicide (though of course the operators are efficient, practical and helpful), the narrator directly asks the reader a rhetorical question about the machine and its eye: "Did it drink of the darkness? Did it suck out all the poisons accumulated with the years?" (p. 15) On the oneiric level of material imagination, we must imagine through this critical negation of technology how time has stopped flowing toward the future for Mildred, how it has gathered in a "liquid melancholy" (p. 17) that cannot be sucked away by the machine, indeed that the "eye" of the machine cannot even see. Unlike the machine and its operators, we must give a full human response, cognitive and sublimative, if we are to grasp the significance of the scene.

Clarisse's disappearance brings about "vague stirrings of dis-ease" (p. 34) in Montag and in a scene in the firehouse he recognizes that these men whose faces are sunburnt by a thousand real and ten thousand imaginary fires are "all mirror images of himself" (p. 35). Montag had stolen a book of fairy tales at the last fire; in a slip of the tongue which reveals the dominance of the anima in his mind he asks Fire Chief Beatty if "once upon a time" firemen put out fires instead of lighting them (p. 36). This brings on a lesson in history of the Fireman of America which is nothing less than an illustration of the Freudian dream-work, which distorts a basic content in order to represent a wish as fulfilled. Benjamin Franklin is the founding father who established the Firemen in the colonies to burn English-influenced books. The lives of the Firemen are governed by a series of five rules laid down by him that define a narrative circuit from alarm to fire to firehouse to alarm, the very instance of an anxiety mechanism.

In the next fire Montag witnesses a suicide that is undertaken deliberately with full knowledge of the consequences. An old woman chooses to die in the conflagration which destroys her library and home rather than be taken to the insane asylum. This action, while it horrifies Montag, also leads him to equate people with books and books with people. Fire Chief Beatty argues that the old woman was driven insane by the contradictions among the books ("a regular damned Tower of Babel" p. 41), but Montag begins to realize that their job is only to provide more spectacle, a show for the neighbors (p. 42). In addition to this cognitive level of discovery, the oneiric level of significance emerges when books begin to pour out of the destroyed walls of the house onto Montag's shoulders:

"A book lit, almost obediently, like a white pigeon, in his hands, wings fluttering. In the dim, wavering light, a page hung open and it was like a snowy feather, the words delicately painted thereon." (p. 39). This is a clear image of transcendence, the bird being symbolic of a proffered flight to the imaginary. The feather is snowy and of a very different climate from the burning world with which Montag is familiar. And the words of this book are not printed, making it a symbol of technology, but *painted,* which suggests the medieval illumination of manuscripts where words themselves come alive in ornate and painfully slow scriptive fantasy. Once one has seen one of these books, all other books, however produced, pale in comparison. Unfortunately, Montag loses this book of reveries, but not before reading a line in it: "Time has fallen asleep in the afternoon sunshine" (p. 40), which suggests an illuminator patiently reading and transcribing with love a sacred scripture, an occasion on which real time would seem to be transformed magically. It is nonetheless a powerful negation of Montag's sense of time as burning away the past and memory and history.

It is no wonder then that Montag is not ready to accept Fire Chief Beatty's defense of the status quo, no matter how sympathetic he may seem. His perspective is undercut by all we and Montag have learned about books. They may indeed by contradictory, but that experience in itself is somehow valuable. Beatty wants a type of society that requires only enough mind to create and tend machines, which, of course, he thinks are marvelous labor-saving devices. He thinks that they have eliminated unhappiness: "The zipper displaces the button and a man lacks just that much time to think while dressing at dawn, a philosophical hour, and thus a melancholy hour" (p. 59). It is, of course, also an indication of his ambivalence towards the "doubleness" of philosophy whose terms seem to keep sliding despite the quest to embody truth, and an ironic indictment of him, that his own speech reveals more than he intends it to, that it is more than just the revelation that "Technology, mass exploitation, and minority pressure did the trick," (p. 61) in bringing about this "happy society." Beatty's language is an attempt to "sell" Montag on the idea of being a fireman, which is why it seems to be alienated from any connected meaning or attempt to think of a social totality. Just before he launches into his defense, we see him obsessively flicking his lighter:

> He examined his eternal matchbox, the lid of which said GUARANTEED: ONE MILLION LIGHTS IN THIS LIGHTER, and began to strike the chemical match abstractedly, blow out, strike, blow out, strike, speak a few words, blow out. He looked at the flame. He blew, he looked at the smoke. "When will you be well?" (p. 57)

This brief passage informs the reader about how to imagine the relationship between consciousness, language, and its objects during the course of Beatty's speech. It shows us the lighter as a practical technological device bearing a promise, but this object in turn shows us only the reified language of mass culture itself.

The lighter is a fetish, an emblem of the eternal consumer, the ideal of this society of narcissists (in contrast, Faber tells Montag: "I don't talk *things*, sire. . . I talk the *meaning* of things." (p. 81). So the structure of Beatty's language, and the reasons for its debasement, are here succinctly presented for the reader. As a symbol of our control over fire, with its promise of a million imaginary fires, it must be understood in a negative sense. Its ideal, the beauty in consumption, is a deception, based on repitition and sameness. It is this deception we must bear in mind throughout Beatty's defense and in the next part of the novel where we again see him talking about the "false promises" (p. 83) that literature offers.

Beatty's language has a quality difficult to capture in brief quotation. It seems to destroy previous stages of the argument without preserving anything for further thought. Although it is full of novelty and dynamic tempo (he invokes a film speeding faster and faster), it is really governed by a constant sameness, the rhythm of mechanical reproduction. It is a montage of superstructural effects which do not touch upon basic economic realities. Beatty's attitude towards the past (which he is supposed to be revealing) is obviously one in which there is no possible experience of an integrated tradition. Everything has to run incessantly to maintain the illusion of life:

> "Speed up the film, Montag, quick. *Click, Pic, Look, Eye, Now, Flick, Here, There, Swift, Pace, Up, Down, In, Out, Why, How, Who, What, Where, Eh?, Uh! Bang! Smack! Wallop, Bing, Bong, Boom!* Digests-digests, digest-digest-digests. Politics? One column, two sentences, a headline! Then, in midair, all vanishes! Whirl man's mind around so fast under the pumping hands of publishers, exploiters, broadcasters that the centrifuge flings off all unnecessary, time-wasting thought! (p. 59)

This is really a biting satire about the ways in which the culture industry turns the successes of enlightenment into mass deception. With the proliferation of magazines does not come more knowledge and power for the individual, but the absence of these things, and a brutalization and re-barbarization of language, a gradual descent into subhuman grunts. The lack of political discussion indicates that real freedom has been forfeited in order to preserve happiness (political candidates are chosen for their "winning images," (p. 105). There is nothing left for the consumer to classify, no fundamental concepts that are evoked by these pre-digested tabloids. Beatty gives an artifical impression of being in command, but as he stares abstractedly into his eternal consumer lighter, we know that he is simply rationalizing. We must seek out, as Montag does, the true utopian wise man, Faber, who appears in the second part of the novel.

Part II, "The Sieve and the Sand," foregrounds the process of reading itself as a process of self-discovery. Once he begins reading in earnest, Montag is deeply worried that he will not be able to retain what he has read (hence the sieve), or understand it more deeply. He therefore seeks out an old retired school teacher, Faber. During this search the programmed fantastic is intensified as a threat to reading (especially pp. 85-86, in the subway). But finally Montag is equipped by Faber with an electronic transmitter which allows them to communicate their thoughts and especially for Faber to read to him unbeknownst to others. But Montag rashly thinks that he can reform his wife and her friends at one of their T.V. parlor parties by reading them a poem (Arnold's "Dover Beach"). This event marks the turning point of the novel, for Montag is now in open rebellion. Although he tries to cover up his mistake by burning the book in question, and even though he appears to lose another debate with Beatty, his wife decides to turn in the alarm on him. Part II ends with the fire engine arriving at Montag's own house. Again the oneiric level of the text provides us with instructions about how to imagine these events. In particular, Faber's demystifying of the pro- grammed fantastic occurs before we are given a series of representations from it (earlier we were only given the fragmented experience of the self in such a fantasy, p. 48), which provides us with the proper distantiation to effect a criticism of its inner mechanisms and the secret of its appeal.

Early on in this part Montag remembers or imagines Beatty telling him how to read a book:

> He could hear Beatty's voice. "Sit down, Montag. Watch. Delicately, like the petals of a flower. Light the first page, light the second page. Each becomes a black butterfly. Beautiful, eh? Light the third page from the second and so on, chain smoking, chapter by chapter, all the silly things the words mean, all the false promises, all the second-hand notions and time-worn philosophies." There sat Beatty, perspiring gently, the floor lit- tered with swarms of black moths that had died in a single storm. (p. 83)

Beatty's reading is a kind of defloration, a perverse destruction that con- serves nothing but depends on a total blank out of differences, lighting the third page from the second, never achieving synthesis but destroying past stages of history. The delicate nuances of meaning (color) produced by the flowering of reverie in the reader's mind (recall the flower image offered by the narrator of "The Sea Shell" here) are homogenized and made black by fire. Fire destroys those impurities and frictions, those irritants in reading that stimulate us to discover new things. Fire destroys dialectical negation, the very principle of reading, as Iser has shown, and with it the labor of the concept and the fruit- fulness of historical contradiction. The hallucination Beatty creates on the basis of the text is one of repetition and sameness. Each page becomes a black moth in the scattering storm of his reading. The butterfly, often a symbol of fantasy itself, or, in less capricious terms, of the soul's unconscious attraction towards light, here dies without the hope of ever rising up past the threshold of the unconscious, for Beatty's reading is a habituation, like chain smoking. Elsewhere, in a later perspective segment bearing on his fascination for fire, Beatty says:

> "What is there about fire that's so lovely? No matter what age we are, what draws us to

it?'' Beatty blew out the flame and lit it again. "It's perpetual motion; the thing man wanted to invent but never did. Or almost perpetual motion. If you let it go on, it'd burn our lifetimes out. What is fire? It's a mystery. Scientists give us gobbledegook about friction and molecules. But they don't really know. Its real beauty is that it destroys responsibility and consequences. A problem gets too burdensome, then into the furnace with it. Now, Montag, you're a burden. And fire will lift you off my shoulders, clean, quick, sure; nothing to rot later. Antibiotic, aesthetic, practical.'' (p. 125)

Here Beatty's feeling for the beauty of fire, which mingles elements of both idolatry and ideology, belies his interest in its supposedly technological and practical effects. He is drawn to it (like a moth) because it destroys responsibility for his own life, his freedom. We note the persistence of a mythical attitude despite his claims to enlightenment. He even claims to know what the positivists do not know about fire with their "gobbledegook": fire as ideology is not brought about by friction with the real.

As Bachelard has shown, fire is an imaginative force that constantly distorts scientific inductions because it can explain anything—that is the secret of its ambivalence, which can never be entirely mastered, for human desires. It is both the subject (that which burns) and object (that which is burned); it is love, it is hate, comfort and torture, cookery and apocalypse.[28] Beatty reveals his awareness of these contradictions when he says that fire is antibiotic, aesthetic, and practical, yet still a mystery, all at the same time. But if by ideology is meant a particular or relative discourse seeking to pass itself off as universal or absolute, then Beatty's discourse deserves this title, for it affirms only certain aspects of fire—those which stabilize a society of spectacles (the phoenix emblem on his uniform is a perfect example of this). Instead of proving our domination over nature, Beatty's discourse reveals an alienated nature's power over him, for man could never invent perpetual motion, the ideal of the consumer culture.

Beatty's complex thus is a true complex uniting the love of fire with the instinct for dying, felt as the appeal of the flames. At the center of his idolatry of fire is the Empedocles complex (Bachelard's name for it) containing the wish for the least lonely of deaths, one that would involve the entire universe in a conflagration (yes, Beatty also wants a cosmic reverie), but ironically he dies the most dehumanizing of deaths.[29] In addition and most importantly, Beatty's idolatry of fire embraces the very principle of consumer culture: repetition and mechanical reproduction; once the reader discovers this, he has realized Bradbury's implicit oneiric criticism of our society.

It is Faber, however, who instructs Montag in the phenomenology of the reading process:

"Number one: Do you know why books such as this are so important? Because they have quality. And what does the word quality mean? To me it means texture. This book has *pores*. It has features. This book can go under the microscope. You'd find life under the glass, streaming past in infinite profusion. The more pores, the more truthfully recorded details of life per square inch you can get on a sheet of paper, the more 'literary' you are. That's *my* definition anyway. *Telling detail. Fresh* detail. The good writers touch life often. The mediocre ones run a quick hand over her. The bad ones rape her and leave her for the flies.

"So now do you see why books are hated and feared? They show the pores in the face of life. The comfortable people want only wax moon faces, poreless, hairless, expressionless. We are living in a time when flowers are trying to live on flowers, instead of growing on good rain and black loam. Even fireworks, for all their prettiness, come from the chemistry of the earth. Yet somehow we think we can grow, feeding on flowers and fireworks, without completing the cycle back to reality." (p. 90)

The forbidden and dangerous book that Faber is holding in his hands—the Bible—could well stand as a resonant symbol for the totality of literature, so many of the central myths and archetypal patterns of literature have come from it (including both patterns of utopia, the arcadian paradise and the heavenly city). According to Northrop Frye, the Bible is a total verbal order, the supreme example of how various myths can be integrated into a single vast vision of the world. Faber asserts almost the same thing earlier in this dialogue when he says the magic in the web of literature is texture: "How they stitched the patches of the universe into one garment for us" (p. 90).

Indeed, there is a striking resemblance between Faber's remarks on the function of literature and Frye's assertion that the reader himself is responsible for the moral quality of what he reads, that the cultivated response to culture is a redemptive if not a revolutionary act of consciousness. Faber is a kind of failed Northrop Frye, who has always insisted that we can get a whole liberal education simply by picking up one conventional poem and following its archetypes as they stretch out into the rest of literature. In the context of a study of romance (which Frye believes to be the structural core of all fiction) Frye remarks:

> When we study the classics of literature, from Homer on, we are following the dictates of common sense, as embodied in the author of Ecclesiastes: 'Better is the sight of the eye than the wandering of desire.' Great literature is what the eye can see: it is the genuine infinite as opposed to the phony infinite, the endless adventures and endless sexual stimulation of the wandering of desire.[30]

This resemblance may seem all the more striking when we remember that Montag's moral response to this society, which stimulates the wanderings of desire, is, loving the wisdom of the preacher so much, to become the Book of Ecclesiastes among the itinerant book people.

Actually, Frye is ambivalent about the wanderings of desire, as of any centrifugal motion. Perhaps, he opines, literature would not exist without it, for the production of culture may be, like ritual, a half-involuntary imitation of organic rhythms or processes. But our response to *culture* remains nevertheless a formed response to human values. For Frye, literature is not mere wish-fulfillment; it provides not satisfaction of desire, but a realization of both its positive and negative moments (in *Fahrenheit 451,* for example, the reader discovers both the negative and positive dimensions of utopia). The literary universe is saturated with desire: its heroes incarnate the desirable, its villains the undesirable. The romance-world, and by extension the world of literature in general, is a paradise, then, not because our desires are always fulfilled there, but because they can in any case always be incarnated, brought to consciousness, formulated by the reader. For Faber also fiction is a genuine infinite, an imaginative vision that is also an ordering process, opposed by its very structure to the spectacles (fireworks) of the mass media.

But whereas Frye's visual imagination pertains more to a flash of insight, when we at a certain point in the narrative see a total design or unifying structure of converging significance, and nothing more, Faber's gives way to material imagination and our recessive desire in reading. People have lost touch with the earth, the principle of continuity and reality. They have lost the ability to ground their needs in the experience of satisfaction and real contentment. They have allowed the "helping professions"—psychiatrists, family counselors—to define their needs and psychic health for them. It is no wonder that those needs never seem to be satisfied: they are completely mediated by electronic images; flowers are trying to live on flowers.

Faber's reading complex appreciates images, telling details, but wants them to be part of the chemistry of the earth. Literature must also make us feel Bachelardian reverie, the texture of that good black loam. For him, books smell of nutmeg or some spice from a foreign land: "I loved to smell them when I was a boy" (p. 88). Even though he scoffs at Montag's naive request that he teach him to read, calling him a hopeless romantic for equating books with happiness (the archetypal wise old man always has some sobering truth for us!) he reveals through his reading complex that literature was for him as a boy the secular scripture, romance. Frye suggests that it is possible to look at secular stories as a whole, as forming a single integrated vision of the world, parallel to the Christian and Biblical vision. Faber shares this formal and visual imagination, telling Montag next a story from that other fabulous branch of now secular literature, classical mythology: the fable of Hercules and Antaeus; but the very presence of a book such as the Bible (which he has not held in his hands for so long) is enough to stir the material imagination of a better world.

Faber tells Montag, and us, how to read, by himself using suggestive details. Hercules was only able to defeat the giant wrestler, Antaeus (whose mother was Earth and who stands here for the force of the material imagination) by holding him rootless in the air. Each time Hercules threw Antaeus to the ground he grew stronger from contact with his source, so each time we read books of quality and texture we gain the experience of life—grainy, fibrous, woven and dimensional, as opposed to smooth, narcissistic, surface interests. Faber's Antaeus complex also tells us that as acts of consciousness and as lived experiences, images (flowers/fireworks) produced from the reading process must be sustained by an awareness of a historical dimension. In Iser's cognitive terms we would say that the text's repertoire of literary allusions suggest answers to the problems that the selection of norms and thought systems raises. Realistic texture (Faber's aesthetic is close to that of a realist) is therefore the imaginary correction of a deficient reality. It is an infinite profusion that is imaginatively real, not a false infinity of mere facts. By contrast, Beatty wants people crammed full of "noncombustible data" (p. 65), such as the fact, which every fireman and reader of the book should know, that book paper catches fire at 451° F.

Although this vision of a radiant literacy has failed, in another sense it has not entirely been disproved either, which is perhaps the reason why Montag chooses to read Matthew Arnold's "Dover Beach" to Mildred and her friends in a scene we will examine in a moment. The powers of literature exist apart from any attempt to theorize them, and theory may ultimately be a kind of defense against this power, as Geoffrey Hartman argues in connection with *Fahrenheit 451*.[31] As readers we realize this also about Beatty's theorizing: he is secretly afraid of literature. When Montag is asked by one of Mildred's friends if the presence of the book in his hands is because he is reading up on fireman theory he responds: "Theory, hell. . . It's poetry" (p. 106). So we would be wise to keep our distance from theory as well in reading this book. Nevertheless, we can affirm that Faber, like Frye, still convinces us that we need a means to unite the world of nature with a total human form. Frye has argued that culture insists on totality—for whatever is excluded from culture by religion or state will get its revenge somehow. Faber exults in Montag's ruse of putting forbidden books he has stolen in the houses of firemen and then turning in the alarm: "The salamander devours his tail!" (p. 94). Faber's speech is didactic, but it leaves open paths of reverie and cognition by using the legend of Hercules and Antaeus for Montag to imagine and complete his own cycle back to reality. Books precisely are *not* completely real, although they allow the real to enter into them. They can be beaten down with reason, he says. On the other hand the programmed fantastic is so immediate that it rivals the real world: "It grows you any shape it wishes!" (p. 91).

Let us now consider, in the light of these discoveries made by the utopian reader, an example of the representations of the programmed fantastic:

> "Isn't this show *wonderful*?" cried Mildred.
> "Wonderful!"
> On one wall a woman smiled and drank orange juice simultaneously. How does she do both at once? thought Montag, insanely. In the other walls an x-ray of the same woman revealed the contracting journey of the refreshing beverage on its way to her delighted stomach! Abruptly the room took off on a rocket flight into the clouds, it plunged into a lime-green sea where blue fish ate red and yellow fish. A minute later, Three White Cartoon Clowns chopped off each other's limbs to the accompaniment of immense incoming tides of laughter. Two minutes more and the room whipped out of town to the jet cars wildly circling an arena, bashing and backing up and bashing each other again. Montag saw a

number of bodies fly in the air.
"Millie, did you *see* that!"
"I saw it, I *saw* it!"
Montag reached inside the parlor wall and pulled the main switch. The images drained away, as if the water had been let from a gigantic crystal bowl of hysterical fish. (p. 102)

In the five minutes during the showing of this fantasy, we see more action than in our slow moving world in many a day. It is, in fact, almost a perfect realization of Lasch's fears about the warlike social relations of a declining capitalist society where people are bashing and chopping each other to pieces for more consumer goods. First of all, we note the stimulation of infantile oral cravings. The x-ray provides the assurance (in this society which respects scientific images and facts it creates an aura of authenticity) that the shadowy and specular image of the ideal consumer's satisfaction is real. Then there follows a series of aggressive fantasy scenes, disconnected, and which entertain no relations of any kind with the reality principle. The action in these scenes completely defies the laws of gravitation, and seemingly all other known laws of nature. The room takes off on a rocket flight into the clouds and in the same sentence splashes into a lime-green sea where predation comically takes place. Weirdly artificial colors lend a kind of cartoon beauty to this scene that belies the obvious agression of the fish; this is a reverie of the bright narcissistic surface of water, which quickly disperses without committing the imagination.

As the psychoanalytic critic Hans Sachs wittily observed on the subject of cartoons, this is animation with a vengeance (Sachs was punning on the regression of "animistic" thinking in cartoons).[32] But interestingly, Sachs argued that the cartoon, unlike the fairy tale which does arouse anxiety and enable us to master it through its formal literary properties, is unable to eliminate or even diminish an anxiety situation (caused by the aggressive impulses of the spectator's projected id). This is so, Sachs argued, because in its pure form the cartoon is pure id, the overflowing vitality of libido. It offers us no coherence either of plot or of figures remotely resembling the human and through which we might identify.

How, then, does the cartoonist display so much aggression without arousing anxiety? Basically, says Sachs, it is "the amazing unreality of the world of cartoons which saves us from anxiety."[33] In cartoons there really is no *form* by which we might master our fears (in Holland's sense of the transformation of fantasy), but everything is kept in constant motion (against the known laws of nature) so that our emotions seems sufficiently real, i.e., vivid. The cartoonist uses the unlimited despotic powers afforded to him by his medium to keep anxiety out of it. And as Lasch's social criticism here corroborates, in this type of fantasy Bradbury shows us that the modern propaganda of commodities has no need to disguise its id impulses—it gives us the illusion of a world full of vitality and force (in order to sell orange juice) and without the need for our imagination to engage itself. In the programmed fantastic, there are no novelistic techniques of illusion-building that might seek to simulate the reality of an action or a situation by having the reader use his own "free" imagination. Indeed, the very category of the real seems to be absent.

The Three White Clowns, who merrily chop each other's limbs off, are, of course, human figures, but the unreality of their gestures is rather emphasized by the fact that they are clowns. Anxiety is not supposed to be aroused here because they are not really losing their limbs (Sachs provides the example of Mickey Mouse, who in one instant is cut in half by a rolling wheel with a razor edge, and who in the next instant is reunited again, none the worse for his experience) in this unmistakably sadistic situation. It may of course arouse anxiety in the reader of *Fahrenheit 451*, but that is another matter. The spectators of this fantasy are perfectly assured that this violence is not real because the one technique for displacing anxiety that cartoons do in fact have is here effectively used: the Three White Clowns chop off each other's limbs to the accompaniment of immense incoming tides of *laughter*.

After unplugging the T.V. walls, Montag reads to Mildred and her friends Matthew Arnold's "Dover Beach." It is an indication of Bradbury's confidence in the power of literature to bring neglected states of mind to light, to convert passive knowledge into active, that he makes us feel in this scene, despite the obvious impracticality of Montag's gesture, that as long as we remember one poem from the repertoire of mankind's greatest poetry, the effects of habituation which threaten to devour, like fire, our families, friends, and even our fear of war, will find it more difficult to settle in. The last line about ignorant armies clashing by night rings particularly true for this society which indeed seems like a land of dreams, for none of the women seem to acknowledge the impending war. The poem provides also the idea of an alternative life in which people really speak to one another. Lovers communicate their deepest feelings, needs, and aspirations consequent on the very condition of being alive, knowing they have to die, needing love. This is decidedly not the happy ending which these women have come to expect, however, for it brings out uncontrollable sobbing in Mrs. Phelps and outright anger in Mrs. Bowles. Montag cannot help furiously throwing them out of his house when they attack him for arousing real emotions in them.

He realizes later that he has made a terrible error in acting so openly against the state and reproaches himself for being such a fool. Nevertheless, as Faber gradually reads to him he feels himself gently split into two people, one of whom is educating the other. On the oneiric level of experience, Montag is able to imagine himself as fire plus water, Montag-plus-Faber: "Out of two separate and opposite things, a third" (p. 112). That third thing brought about by dialectical sublimation is wine, for wine remembers, as it is put away and conserved, the earth from which it came. This new self will remember the past and will know the fool it once was.

It is only in part III, "Burning Bright," that technology is used directly against itself. Montag destroys the mechanical hound with a "single wondrous

blossom" of fire (p. 130), and Beatty as well, who dies like "a gibbering manne-
kin, no longer human or known" (p. 130). Montag also burns his own house,
making everything once familiar seem strange. In a final nightmarish scene,
Montag on the run has a vision of himself reflected in millions of T.V. sets, and
imagines seeing himself killed on television by the hound, "a drama to be watched
objectively" (p. 146). This vision of a fictive self and its false identification with
society marks the climax of Montag's feelings of unreality and doubleness. From
hence forth in the novel burning bright will mean the rediscovery of the utopian
ideal. We need now to examine how this is presented to the reader:

> He felt as if he had left a stage behind and many actors. He felt as if he had left the great
> seance and all the murmuring ghosts. He was moving from an unreality that was frighten-
> ing into a reality that was unreal becasue it was new. (p. 152).

The narrator relates these thoughts of Montag as he is "floating in a sudden
peacefulness" downstream in a very real river he has plunged into in order to
escape pursuit by the mechanical hound and the helicopters. They mark the
beginning of a transition, a rebirth through water, a rite of passage that divests
Montag entirely of his Fireman persona. This long water reverie symbolically
puts out all the imaginary fires in Montag's mind. Montag's reverie becomes
cosmic when he dreams of the sun and the burning of Time and the moon which
shines by reflected light, discovering that he must never burn again in his life if
human time is to be preserved.

When Montag drifts toward the shore, another reverie begins, organizing
and transforming Montag's experience toward a utopian openness to the future.
It has a highly organized, complexly layered, existential structure bearing the
three dimensions of time (one indication that the programmed fantastic is so
unreal is that it does not possess these existential temporal horizons): including
the rediscovery of a happy childhood memory, events in the present, and a situation which is to emerge in the future, representing the fulfillment of a utopian
wish as a broken promise.

The motion of the waters and the smell of hay from the shore awaken in
Montag the memory of a farm he visited when he was "very young, one of the
rare few times he discovered that somewhere behind the seven veils of unreality,
beyond the tin moat of the city, cows chewed grass and pigs sat in warm ponds at
noon, and dogs barked after white sheep on a hill" (p. 154). Obviously, he has
transformed and idealized this memory through reverie into an arcadian utopia.
Montag imagines sleeping in a hay loft on that farm. From this inhabited space he
projects images of the future, utopian longings:

> During the night, he thought, below the loft, he would hear a sound like feet moving,
> perhaps. He would tense and sit up. The sound would move away. He would lie back and
> look out the loft window, very late in the night, and see the lights go out in the farmhouse

itself, until a very young and beautiful woman would sit in an unlit window, braiding her hair. It would be hard to see her, but her face would be like the face of the girl so long ago in his past now, so very long ago, the girl who had known the weather and never been burnt by the fireflies, the girl who had known what dandelions meant rubbed off on your chin. Then, she would be gone from the warm window and appear again upstairs in her moon-whitened room. And then, to the sound of death, the sound of the jets cutting the sky in two black pieces beyond the horizon, he would lie in the loft, hidden and safe, watching those strange new stars over the rim of the earth, fleeing from the soft color of dawn. (pp. 154-155)

Because of its oneiric level of meaning, this passage bears an experience of exceptional poignance. It may even approach the sublime. All the elements of its structure seem braided together like the girl's hair, with loving recollection. Clarisse has disappeared, and Montag hopes that she is not dead, projecting her face on that of the very beautiful young woman he imagines distantly in the window. That woman is clearly archetypal, however, being a Jungian spirit figure who symbolizes the free and sovereign image-making capacity of the mind. Clarisse had revealed Montag's unhappy being to him through the being of an image, a "dandelion test." She seems to him now the very spirit of utopia, innocent and inviolate, never burned by the sparks of any destructive fire, enabling him to master the sound of death with her fairy-tale stillness and beauty, helping him to watch with the ease of reverie the dawn chase away the apocalyptic stars.

For Freud, the utopian urge originates in the drive to restore an earlier state of gratification (mother-infant Eden-eternity), but Montag's reverie, from which we are forced to make only this brief selection, is actually what Ernst Bloch describes as a *Traum nach vorwarts,* a dreaming forward which fills the future with sublimated images of utopian desire. These images are certainly compounded of childhood wishes and desires, but reverie has so idealized them that they are uplifting and inspiring, quite unlike the images of satisfaction that can be found in the programmed fantastic, which are narcissistic and destructive. According to Bloch, the essence of the utopian principle is this: the interweaving of fear and wish (in our case, activated by the childhood image of the dawn) into a visionary future modeled on remembrance, imaginary or partially real, of the past. But Bloch stresses that utopian desire is not chaotic; it is *formed* wish. We would say that it is an imaginative existential structure open to the future: ". . . for the day-dreaming 'I' persists throughout, consciously, privately, envisaging the circumstances and images of a desired, better life."[34]

Montag's reverie is therefore a means for overtaking the future rather than a regression to the past. This scene resonates with what Bloch calls aurora archetypes which, when examined hermeneutically, reveal indications of utopian content like a glow on the horizon. For example, consider the open window lit by moonlight (which, we have already learned from Montag's cognitive reverie in Part 1, shines with a reflected light, reminding us of a source of light to come) where we can barely see the face of our ideal. Consider the girl herself who symbolizes utopian reverie and who remains forever young despite the fact that Montag knows that Clarisse is dead (hence the feeling of broken promise in the passage). And finally, there is the dawn itself, which we are certain is going to bring the apocalypse yet not entirely destroy our hopes for the future.

Objects too are transformed in this reverie, revealing their being to us. Montag' reverie is powered by distinctly oral images of happiness, yet paradoxically these objects are not there to be destroyed by eating; they are signs of a different relationship to the world:

> A cool glass of fresh milk, and a few apples and pears laid at the foot of the steps. This was all he wanted now. Some sign that the immense world would accept him and give him the long time he needed to think all the things that must be thought. (p. 155)

Imagining this scene, Montag steps from the river, having gained some notion of what the real satisfaction of human needs must be like ". . . a complete country night would have rested and slept him while his eyes were wide and his mouth, when he thought to test it, was half a smile" (p. 155). In the pink light of early morning when Montag has been made so aware of the world through his reverie, these objects appear as a "small miracle." But they are more than just the signs of a new composure towards things. Since they are no longer objects for consumption, allowing for their being to be revealed, Montag wants the time to "think all the things that need to be thought" in the hope of a poetic dwelling on the earth. Only when we let the thing *be* as the gathering together of the world in its "worlding" do we think, Heidegger says, of the thing as thing, how all that a thing is, is granted to it by the world.[35] In terms of Heidegger's phenomenology, the fruit and the glass of milk a "thinging" things, not objects consigned to oblivion of being by technological thinking. These objects have lost their aura of commodity production and have taken on the power to reveal our being-in-the-world.

It is difficult to summarize the many levels of Montag's utopian aspirations in this long water reverie, and we have not even touched upon his dream of inhabiting the hayloft which stabilizes him long enough to participate in dramatic cosmic events, to represent to himself a world which is as yet to him unexplored and unfamiliar (he is floating on the surface of the water during the entire sequence). As an ontological structure relating self and world, however, we can affirm that it clearly manifests what Paul Tillich calls the transcendence of utopia: a structure of being wanting to transcend itself although at the same time wanting to remain within itself and protect itself.[36] Montag's imaginary house-barn is a well-rooted being, so he does not fear climbing up to the loft where he can be open to the wind and the dawn, and to another house seen from outside at night.[37]

Montag goes on, after he emerges from the river, to deeper reveries of a new autochthony in the forest world, where he imagines himself an animal attracted to a campfire, around which a group of the itinerant book-people have gathered to warm themselves. Montag is unfamiliar with this human use of fire and with the experience of language it gives rise to:

> There was a silence gathered all about the fire and the silence was in the men's faces, and time was there, time enough to sit by this rusting track under the trees and look at the world and turn it over with the eyes, as if it were held to the center of the bonfire, a piece of steel these men were all shaping. It was not only the fire that was different. It was the silence. Montag moved toward this special silence that was concerned with all of the world.
>
> And then the voices began and they were talking, and he could hear nothing of what the voices said, but the sound rose and fell quietly and the voices were turning the world over and looking at it; the voices knew the land and the trees and the city which lay down the track by the river. The voices talked of everything, there was nothing they could not talk about, he knew, from the very cadence and motion and continual stir of curiosity and wonder in them. (pp. 158-59)

This description of campfire and silence at first breaks the pattern of narrative by putting the reader in a position of reverie, and therefore of reflection vis-à-vis himself. It is, in fact, a Bachelardian reverie of the forge which expresses the liberation of natural resources and the productive use of human energies.[38] These men are intent on touching the world in material imagination, shaping it like a piece of metal in the sunset of their fire. Concern is the dominant mood. Even though we enter into a position of observing, we do not lose ourselves through technological domination of nature, because language and representation here arise from a conscious center (the bonfire). New worlds are being cast; language has the power to talk about anything but nothing is repressed. In the image of the campfire-forge, Bradbury shows us how the imagination (for it is clear that Montag has never before encountered such a "forge" in reality) can itself provide standards and values for our involvement with the world.

Even the nightmare of the telescreens has shrunk to a manageable proportion in this wilderness:

> Granger snapped the portable viewer on. The picture was a nightmare, condensed, easily passed from hand to hand in the forest, all whirring color and flight. (p. 160)

It is Granger who further enlightens Montag about the programmed fantastic by showing him how to view, without allowing his imagination to take over, the death of someone who unfortunately looks like him on the telescreen. He exposes this society's carefully controlled scapegoating and murder of innocent victims. We realize that books have been the mock victims on an altar of fiery sacrifice all along. This society was not rational or enlightened, but had reverted to myth and ritual in order to control forces it no longer understood.

After the atomic war that has been building finally erupts, destroying the city, Granger also tells Montag a fable about the phoenix, who "must have been a first cousin to man" (p. 177). This is not symbolism, but allegory. The fabulous bird embodies our multi-colored dreams of the dominance of nature — our aspiration towards utopia — but also the destructive tendencies inherent in such a project which involves a forgetting of ourselves as part of nature. Yet it is also that within us which enables us to overcome the death of our dreams and to build again. *If* we understand it as allegory, we can effect some distance from this blind destructive cycle. The bird is only first cousin to man, and unlike the bird, we know the "damn silly things" we have done as Granger makes clear. We know temporal difference and irony, if we remember our past, our books. Beatty (whose very name suggests the ringmaster of a famous circus) was obsessed with the phoenix and the salamander as visionary images of atemporal authority and power that suppresses differences. We understand now that he was himself a frustrated romantic who believed, despite himself, in numinous symbols of nature.

Montag searches the faces of the book people for some trace of his ideal of radiant literacy, but finds none (p. 168). The old romantic metaphor of the lamp is put away for Granger's idea of the book as a mirror. But we know this is not to be taken to mean simple identification, for we are to take a long hard look at ourselves. Besides, we are jokingly told not to judge a book by its cover. We must read it slowly and thoughtfully first, paying attention to its images and what it has to say. Montag is only partly sure that he has wisdom within him, but not from the tree of knowledge. As the book ends we are offered a quotation from Revelations that is itself a leaf from the tree of life, for the healing of nations. Knowledge must someday be converted back into life; through it the fruitfulness of utopia must come.

The complaint that utopian novels are more concerned with ideas than characters, and present characters who are simply one-dimensional spokesmen for the author's social hypothesis, is often voiced. I do not think that this change can be brought successfully against *Fahrenheit 451,* despite the fact that it uses the conventional figures of the utopian novel (Montag is himself the utopian traveller in disguise). Because it dramatizes the contradictions of books in a society where the reading of literature is forbidden, it motivates the reader easily and intensely to take up the quest for the utopian past. And because of its suggestive deployment of many different modes of reverie, it preserves the archetypes of utopian satisfaction as a criticism of the culture industry the reading subject has to work out for himself. Is it necessary to say that *Fahrenheit 451* continues to be relevant today, since the trends Bradbury projected in 1953 are unabated?

Notes

Introduction

1. For an early example, see Christopher Isherwood, "Review of *The Martian Chronicles,*" *Tomorrow* (Oct., 1950), pp. 56-58.

2. Tzvetan Todorov, *The Fantastic,* trans. Richard Howard (Ithaca: Cornell University Press, 1975), p. 89.

3. Ibid., p. 82.

4. Eric S. Rabkin, *The Fantastic in Literature* (Princeton: Princeton University Press, 1976), p. 164.

5. W. R. Irwin, *The Game of the Impossible* (Urbana: University of Illinois Press, 1976), p. 9.

6. Darko Suvin, *Metamorphoses of Science Fiction* (New Haven: Yale University Press, 1979), p. 68.

7. Eric S. Rabkin, *A Reader's Guide to Arthur C. Clarke* (Mercer Island: Starmont House, 1979), p. 28.

8. Georg Lukacs, *Writer and Critic,* trans. Arthur D. Kahn (New York, Grosset and Dunlap, 1970), p. 78.

9. Robert Scholes and Eric S. Rabkin, *Science Fiction: History, Science, Vision* (New York: Oxford Univ. Press, 1977), p. 65.

10. Eric S. Rabkin, "To Fairyland by Rocket: Bradbury's *The Martian Chronicles,*" in *Ray Bradbury,* eds. Martin H. Greenburg and Joseph D. Olander (New York: Taplinger, 1980), pp. 111-12.

11. Max Lüthi, *Once Upon a Time,* trans. Lee Chadeayne and Paul Gottwald (Bloomington: Indiana University Press, 1976), p. 52.

12. J. R. R. Tolkien, "On Fairy-Stories," in *The Tolkien Reader* (New York: Ballantine Books, 1966), pp. 58-59.

13. F. C. Fredericks, "Problems of Fantasy," *Science Fiction Studies,* 5 (1978), p. 37.

14. Robert Scholes, "Cognition and the Implied Reader," *Diacritics,* Vol. 5, No. 3 (Fall 1975), p. 14.

15. Mark Rose, ed., *Science Fiction, A Collection of Critical Essays* (Englewood Cliffs: Prentice-Hall, Inc., 1976), p. 4.

16. Gaston Bachelard, *L'Eau et les rêves* (Paris: Corti, 1963), p. 68.

17. Edgar Allan Poe, *Complete Tales and Poems* (New York: Vintage Books, 1975), p. 852.

18. Gaston Bachelard, *On Poetic Imagination and Reverie,* trans. Colette Gaudin (New York: Bobbs-Merrill, 1971), p. 58.

19. Ibid., p. 59.

20. Gaston Bachelard, *Le Droit de rêver* (Paris: P. U. F., 1976), p. 148.

21. Wolfgang Iser, *The Implied Reader* (Baltimore: Johns Hopkins University Press, 1974), p. 232.

Chapter 1

1. Wolfgang Iser, *The Act of Reading* (Baltimore: Johns Hopkins University Press, 1978), p. 38.

2. These remarks are a summary of those given by Booth himself in an exchange with Iser in *Diacritics,* Vol. 10, No. 2 (June 1980), pp. 66-69.

3. W. R. Irwin, *The Game of the Impossible,* p. 183.

4. Norman N. Holland, *The Dynamics of Literary Response* (New York: W. W. Norton, 1975), pp. 31-62.

5. Norman N. Holland, *Poems in Persons* (New York: W. W. Norton, 1973), p. 77.

6. Robert H. Stacy, *Defamiliarization in Language and Literature* (Syracuse: Syracuse University Press, 1977).

7. Maurice Merleau-Ponty, *Signs,* trans. Richard C. McCleary (Evanston: Northwestern University, 1964), p. 54.

8. Iser, *The Act of Reading,* p. 85.

9. Ibid., pp. 98-99.

10. Wolfgang Iser, *The Implied Reader,* p. 285.

11. Ibid., pp. 196-233.

12. Ibid., p. 293.

13. Ibid. p. 294.

14. Ibid., p. 297.

Chapter 2

1. Wolfgang Iser, *The Implied Reader,* p. 150.

2. Ibid., p. 156.

3. Gaston Bachelard, *On Poetic Imagination and Reverie,* p. 37.

4. Gaston Bachelard, *L'Eau et les rêves,* p. 2.

5. Gaston Bachelard, *Le Matérialisme rationnel* (Paris: P. U. F., 1972), p. 12.

6. Wolfgang Iser, "The Current Situation of Literary Theory: Key Concepts and The Imaginary," *New Literary History,* Vol. XI, No. 1 (Autumn 1979), pp. 1-20.

7. Wolfgang Iser, *The Act of Reading,* p. 150.

8. Gaston Bachelard, *La Terre et les rêveries de la volonte,* (Paris: Corti, 1965), pp. 4-5.

9. Gaston Bachelard, *The Poetics of Space,* trans. Maria Jolas (Boston: Beacon Press, 1969), pp. xviii-xix.

10. Gaston Bachelard, *The Poetics of Reverie,* trans. Daniel Russell (Boston: Beacon Hill Press, 1971), p. 157.

11. Maurice Merleau-Ponty, *The Structure of Behavior,* trans. Alden Fisher (Boston: Beacon Press, 1963), p. 177.

12. Gaston Bachelard, *The Psychoanalysis of Fire,* trans. Alan C. M. Ross (Boston: Beacon Press, 1968), p. 112.

13. Ibid.

14. C. G. Jung, *Psychological Types,* trans. H. G. Baynes (London: Routledge and Kegan Paul), p. 428.

15. Gaston Bachelard, *L'Eau et les rêves,* p. 14.

16. Jolande Jacobi, *Complex, Archetype, Symbol in the Psychology of C. G. Jung,* trans. Ralph Manheim (New York: Pantheon Books, 1959), *passim.*

17. Northrop Frye, *The Anatomy of Criticism* (Princeton: Princeton University Press, 1957), p. 305.

18. Gaston Bachelard, *On Poetic Imagination and Reverie,* p. 17.

19. Norman N. Holland, *The Dynamics of Literary Response* (New York: W. W. Norton, 1975), pp. 189-90.

20. Gaston Bachelard, *La Terre et les rêveries de la volonté,* p. 38.

21. Bachelard, *The Psychoanalysis of Fire,* p.110.

22. Northrop Frye, *The Anatomy of Criticism,* p. 163.

23. Mary Ann Caws, *Surrealism and The Literary Imagination* (The Hague: Mouton, 1966), *passim.*

24. Herbert Marcuse, *Eros and Civilization* (New York: Vintage Books, 1962), p. 145.

25. Ibid., pp. 100, 151, 191.

Chapter 3

1. Ray Bradbury, "The Sea Shell," in *The Fantastic Pulps,* ed. Peter Haining (New York: Vintage Books, 1975), pp. 386-94. All further references are in the text.

2. Tzvetan Todorov, *The Fantastic,* trans. Richard Howard (Ithaca: Cornell University Press, 1975), p. 109.

3. W. II. Auden, *The Enchafèd Flood* (New York: Random House, 1950), pp. 86-87.

4. Gaston Bachelard, *The Poetics of Reverie,* p. 110.

5. Jean-Paul Sartre, *Esquisse d'une théorie des émotions* (Paris: Herman, 1965), pp. 58-59. According to Sartre's phenomenological analysis of emotion, affective consciousness is in general a magical and transformative act. He distinguishes two situations in which emotion

arises. In the first, I shatter the deterministic order of a world I find too difficult by unreflective acts directed at my body as object. In the second, the Other shatters the deterministic order by appearing magical to me.

6. Gaston Bachelard, *The Poetics of Space,* p. 110-11.

7. Todorov, *The Fantastic,* pp. 89-90.

8. Ibid., p. 52.

9. Lahna Diskin, "Bradbury on Children," in *Ray Bradbury,* ed. Martin H. Greenburg and Joseph D. Olander (New York: Taplinger, 1980, pp. 127-55. Diskin explores Bradbury's general view of children and tends to confirm this view as the prevalent one in his work.

Chapter 4

1. Hazel Pierce, "Ray Bradbury and the Gothic Tradition," in *Ray Bradbury,* ed. Joseph D. Olander and Martin H. Greenberg (New York: Taplinger, 1980), p. 173.

2. Gaston Bachelard, *L'Eau et les rêves,* p. 113.

3. Ibid., p. 26.

4. Ibid., p. 114.

5. Daniel Hoffman, *Poe, Poe, Poe, Poe, Poe, Poe, Poe* (New York: Avon Books, 1972), pp. xi-xii.

6. *L'Eau et les rêves,* pp. 110-11.

7. Tzvetan Todorov, *The Fantastic,* p.134.

8. Gaston Bachelard, *The Poetics of Reverie,* p.169.

9. Ibid., pp. 79-80

10. Ray Bradbury, "Cistern" in *Dark Carnival* (Sauk City: Arkham House, 1947), pp. 267-78. All further references are in the text.

11. Gaston Bachelard, *La Terre et les rêveries du repos* (Paris: Corti, 1965), p. 286.

12. Erich Neumann, *The Origins and History of Consciousness* (Princeton: Princeton University Press, 1954), p. 49.

13. Bachelard, *La Terre et les rêveries du repos,* p. 200.

14. Ibid., p. 205.

15. Ibid., p. 200.

16. Ibid., p. 185.

17. Ibid., p. 186.

Chapter 5

1. Charles Elkins and Darko Suvin, "Preliminary Reflections on Teaching Science Fiction Critically," *Science Fiction Studies,* vol. 6, no. 19 (1979), pp. 263-64.

2. Darko Suvin, *Metamorphoses of Science Fiction* (New Haven: Yale University Press, 1979), pp. 63-84.

3. Ibid., p. 79.

4. Ibid., p. 83.

5. Ernst Fischer, *The Necessity of Art,* trans. Anna Bostock (Baltimore: Penguin Books, 1963), pp. 95-100.

6. See, however, his defense of *The Martian Chronicles* as myth in Ray Bradbury, et al., *Mars and the Mind of Man* (New York: Harper and Row, 1973), pp. 17-20.

7. Charles Dobzynski, "Ray Bradbury, fabuliste de notre temps," *Europe,* nos. 139,140 (July-August, 1957), pp. 76-87.

8. Ray Bradbury, "Rocket Children," *The Spectator* (Fall, 1979), p. 4.

9. Gaston Bachelard, *The Poetics of Reverie,* pp. 99-141.

10. Ibid., p. 119.

11. Ibid.

12. Ibid., p. 111.

13. Sigmund Freud, "The Acquisition of Power over Fire," trans. Joan Riviere, reprinted in *Character and Culture.* ed. Philip Rieff (New York: Collier Books, 1973), pp. 294-300.

14. Eric Rabkin, *Fantastic Worlds* (New York: Oxford University Press, 1979), p. 8-10.

15. Gaston Bachelard, *The Psychoanalysis of Fire,* pp. 7-12.

16. Albert Camus, *Le Mythe de Sisyphe* (Paris: Gallimard, 1942), pp. 24-45.

17. James Gunn, *Alternate Worlds* (New York: A & W Visual Library, 1975), pp. 225-239. Using ideas from Sartre and other existentialists, Gunn argues convincingly that science fiction's vision of man is one of philosophical paradox, at once arrogant and humble. Thus in our story the Promethean mission is to steal fire from the sun with a "beggar's cup."

18. Ray Bradbury, "The Golden Apples of the Sun," in *The Golden Apples of the Sun* (New York: Bantam Books, 1970), pp. 164-69. All further references are in the text.

19. Wolfgang Iser, "The Current Situation of Literary Theory. Key Concepts and the Imaginary," *New Literary History,* vol. XI, no. 1 (1979), pp. 19-20.

20. Bachelard, *The Poetics of Reverie,* p. 157.

Chapter 6

1. Richard Gerber, *Utopian Fantasy* (New York: McGraw-Hill, 1973), p. 119.

2. Ibid., p. 120.

3. John Huntington, "Utopian and Anti-Utopian Logic: H. G. Wells and his Successors," *Science Fiction Studies,* vol. 9, part 2, no. 27 (July 1982), p. 137.

4. Ibid., p. 138.

5. Max Horkheimer and Theodor W. Adorno, *Dialectic of Enlightenment,* trans. John Cumming (New York: The Seabury Press, 1972), p. 230.

6. Ibid., p.35.

7. Kingsley Amis, *New Maps of Hell* (New York: Harcourt, Brace and Company, 1960), p. 113.

8. Adorno, *Dialectic of Enlightenment,* p. 140.

9. Donald Watt, "Burning Bright, *Fahrenheit 451* as a Symbolic Dystopia," in *Ray Bradbury,* eds. Olander and Greenberg., pp. 195-213. Peter Sisario, "A Study of the Allusions in Ray Bradbury's *Fahrenheit 451,*" *English Journal* (Feb. 1970), pp. 201-6.

10. Christopher Lasch, *The Culture of Narcissism* (New York: Warner Books, 1979), p. 137-38.

11. Louis Marin, *Utopiques: Jeux d'espaces* (Paris: Minuit, 1973), p. 10 and p. 255.

12. Wolfgang Iser, *The Act of Reading,* pp. 100-101.

13. Ray Bradbury, *Fahrenheit 451* (New York: Ballantine Books, 1979), p. 26. All further references are in the text.

14. W. R. Irwin, *The Game of the Impossible,* p. 76.

15. Ibid., p. 97.

16. Ibid., p. 99.

17. Ibid., p. 8.

18. Donald Watt, "Burning Bright," p. 195.

19. As quoted by Jeffner Allen, "A Husserlian Phenomenology of the Child," *Journal of Phenomenological Psychology,* vol. 6, no. 2 (Spring 76), p. 173.

20. Gaston Bachelard, *La Flamme d'une chandelle* (Paris: P. U. F., 1962), p. 57.

21. Ibid., p. 90.

22. Gaston Bachelard, *The Poetics of Reverie,* p. 164.

23. Ernst Bloch, *A Philosophy of the Future,* trans. John Cumming (New York: Herder and Herder, 1970), pp. 1-8.

24. Jolande Jacobi, *The Psychology of C. G. Jung,* trans. Ralph Manheim, (New Haven: Yale University Press, 1943), pp. 105-40.

25. Bruno Bettelheim, *The Uses of Enchantment* (New York: Vintage Books, 1975), pp. 116-35.

26. Bloch, in Maynard Solomon, ed. *Marxism and Art* (New York: Vintage Books, 1973), p. 579.

27. Ursula LeGuin, *The Language of the Night* (New York: G. P. Putnam's Sons, 1979), pp. 59-71.

28. Gaston Bachelard, *The Psychoanalysis of Fire,* p. 5.

29. Ibid., p. 19.

30. Northrop Frye, *The Secular Scripture* (Cambridge: Harvard University Press, 1976), p. 30.

31. Geoffrey H. Hartman, *The Fate of Reading* (Chicago: University of Chicago Press, 1975), p. 255.

32. Hans Sachs, *The Creative Unconscious* (Cambridge: Sci Art Publishers, 1942), pp. 178-89.

33. Ibid., p. 181.

34. Bloch, in Solomon, *Marxism and Art*, p. 578.

35. Martin Heidegger, *Poetry, Language, Thought,* trans. Albert Hofstadter (New York: Harper and Row, 1971), pp. 165-182.

36. Paul Tillich "Critique and Justification of Utopia," in *Utopias and Utopian Thought,* ed. Frank F. Manuel (Boston: Beacon Press, 1965), pp. 296-309.

37. Gaston Bachelard, *La Terre et les rêveries du repos,* pp. 95-128.

38. Gaston Bachelard, *La Terre et les rêveries de la volonté,* pp. 134-182.

Bibliography

I. Bradbury

A. Books and Pamphlets

The Complete Poems of Bradbury. New York: Ballantine, 1982.
Dandelion Wine. New York: Bantam, 1975.
Dark Carnival (Story collection containing "Cistern"). Sauk City: Arkham House, 1947.
Fahrenheit 451. New York: Ballantine, 1979. New afterword by the author.
The Golden Apples of the Sun (story collection containing "The Golden Apples of the Sun").
    New York: Bantam, 1970.
The Halloween Tree. New York: Alfred A. Knopf, 1972.
I Sing the Body Electric. New York: Bantam, 1971.
The Illustrated Man. New York: Bantam, 1952.
Long After Midnight. New York: Bantam, 1978.
The Machineries of Joy. New York: Bantam, 1965.
The Martian Chronicles. New York: Bantam, 1951.
A Medicine for Melancholy. New York: Bantam, 1960.
The October Country (story collection containing revised version of "The Cistern"). New York:
    Ballantine, 1965.
Pillar of Fire and Other Plays. New York: Bantam, 1975.
R is for Rocket. New York: Bantam, 1965.
S is for Space. New York: Bantam, 1970.
Something Wicked This Way Comes. New York: Bantam, 1963.
The Vintage Bradbury. Introduction by Gilbert Highet. New York: Vintage Books, 1965.
The Wonderful Ice Cream Suit and Other Plays. New York: Bantam, 1972.
Zen and the Art of Writing and *The Joy of Writing: Two Essays.* Santa Barbara: Capra Press,
    1973.

B. Short Fiction

"The Sea Shell." in *The Fantastic Pulps.* Edited and introduction by Peter Haining. New York:
    Vintage, 1975, pp. 386-94.

C. Articles and Essays

"Rocket Children." *The Spectator* (Fall, 1979), p. 4.

"On Going a Journey." in *Mars and the Mind of Man*. Edited by Bruce C. Murray. New York: Harper and Row, 1973.

"Dusk in the Robot Museums: The Rebirth of Imagination." Preface to *Other Worlds, Fantasy and Science Fiction Since 1939*. Special Issue of *MOSAIC,* XIII/3-4 (Spring/Summer, 1980), pp. v-xiv.

D. Selected Criticism

Books

Greenberg, Martin Harry, and Joseph D. Olander, eds. *Ray Bradbury.* Writers of the Twenty-First Century Series. New York: Taplinger Publishing Co., 1980.

Johnson, Wayne L. *Ray Bradbury.* Recognitions Series. Dick Riley, general editor. New York: Frederick Ungar Publishing Co., 1980.

Moskowitz, Sam. *Seekers of Tomorrow, Masters of Modern Science Fiction*. New York: Ballantine, 1967, pp. 351-70.

Nolan, William F. *The Bradbury Companion: A Life and Career History, Photolog, and Comprehensive Checklist of Writings With Facsimilies From Ray Bradbury's Unpublished and Uncollected Work in all Media*. Detroit: Gale Research, 1975.

Slusser, George Edgar. *The Bradbury Chronicles*. The Milford Series, Popular Writers of Today, vol. 4. San Bernardino: Borgo Press, 1977.

Articles

Carrouges, Michel. "Ray Bradbury, les martiens, et nous." *Monde-Nouveau,* 79 (May 1954), pp. 56-63.

Deutsch, Michel. "Ray Bradbury et la poésie du futur." *Critique,* no. 22 (July 1957), pp. 604-11.

Dobzynski, Charles. "Ray Bradbury, fabuliste de notre temps." *Europe,* nos. 139-40 (July-August, 1957), pp. 76-87.

Hienger, Jorg. "The Uncanny and Science Fiction." Translated by Elsa Schieder. *Science Fiction Studies,* vol. 6, no. 18 (1979), pp. 144-52.

Isherwood, Christopher. "Christopher Isherwood Reviews *The Martian Chronicles*." *Tomorrow* (Oct. 1950), pp. 56-58.

Jacobs, Robert. "Interview with Ray Bradbury." *The Writer's Digest,* vol. 55, no. 2 (Feb. 1976), pp. 18-25.

Sisario, Peter. "A Study of the Allusions in Bradbury's *Fahrenheit 451*." English Journal (February 1970), pp. 201-6.

Sullivan, Anita T. "Ray Bradbury and Fantasy." *English Journal* (December 1972), pp. 201-6.

Touponce, William F. "Some Aspects of Surrealism in the Work of Ray Bradbury," *Extrapolation* (Fall, 1984, forthcoming).

Touponce, William F. "The Existential Fabulous: A Reading of Ray Bradbury's 'The Golden Apples of the Sun'." *MOSAIC,* XII/3-4 (Spring/Summer, 1980), pp. 203-18.

Valis, Nöel. "*The Martian Chronicles* and Jorge Luis Borges." *Extrapolation,* vol. 20, no. 1 (Spring 1979), pp. 50-59.

II. Bachelard

A. Books of Criticism by Bachelard

L'Air et les songes, Essai sur l'imagination du movement. 4th ed. Paris: Corti, 1962.

La Dialectique de la durée. 2nd ed. Paris: Presses Univ. de France, 1950.

Le Droit de rêver. Edited by Philippe Garcin. Paris: Presses Univ. de France, 1970.
L'Eau et les rêves, Essai sur l'imagination de la matière. 5th ed. Paris: Corti, 1963.
La Flamme d'une chandelle. 2nd ed. Paris: Presses Univ. de France 1962.
L'Intuition de l'instant. 2nd ed. Paris: Gonthier, 1966.
Lautréamont. Paris: Corti, 1939.
Le Matérialisme rationnel. Paris: Presses Univ. de France, 1953.
The Poetics of Space. Translated by Maria Jolas. Boston: Beacon Press, 1969.
The Poetics of Reverie. Translated by Daniel Russell. Boston: Beacon Press, 1971.
The Psychoanalysis of Fire. Translated by Alan C. M. Ross. Boston: Beacon Press, 1968.
La Terre et les rêveries du repos. Essai sur les images de l'intimité. 4th ed. Paris: Corti, 1965.
La Terre et les rêveries de la volonté. Essai sur l'imagination des forces. 4th ed. Paris: Corti, 1965.

B. Books about Bachelard

Caws, Mary Ann. *Surrealism and the Literary Imagination, A Study of Breton and Bachelard.* Paris: Mouton, 1966.
Champigny, Robert. "Gaston Bachelard." in *Modern French Criticism, From Proust and Valéry to Structuralism.* Edited by John K. Simon. Chicago: University of Chicago Press, 1972, pp. 175-91.
Dagognet, Francois. *Gaston Bachelard, sa vie, son oeuvre, avec un resumé de sa philosophie.* Paris: Presses Univ. de France, 1965.
Ehrmann, Jacques. "Introduction to Gaston Bachelard." In *Velocities of Change, Critical Essays from MLN.* Edited by Richard Macksey. Baltimore: Johns Hopkins University Press, 1974, pp. 253-59.
Gagey, Jacques. *Gaston Bachelard ou la conversion à l'imaginaire.* Paris: Marcel Rivere et Cie, 1969.
Gaudin, Colette. *On Poetic Imagination and Reverie, Selections From the Works of Gaston Bachelard.* Edited, translated and introduction by Colette Gaudin. New York: Bobbs-Merrill, 1971.
Ginestier, Paul. *Pour connâitre la penseé de Bachelard.* Paris: Bordas, 1968.
Kushner, Eva M. "The Critical Method of Gaston Bachelard." in *Myth and Symbol, Critical Approaches and Applications.* Edited by Bernice Slote. Lincoln: University of Nebraska Press, 1963, pp. 39-50.
Lecourt, Dominique. *Bachelard, le jour et la nuit.* Paris: Bernard Grasset, 1974.
_____. *L'Épistémologie historique de Gaston Bachelard.* Paris: Vrin, 1969.
_____. *Pour une critique de l'épistémologie.* Paris: Maspero, 1972.
Mansuy, Michel. *Gaston Bachelard et les éleménts.* Paris: Corti, 1967.
Margolin, Jean-Claude. *Bachelard.* Paris: Seuil, 1974.
Naud, Julien. *Structure et sens du symbole, L'Imaginaire chez Gaston Bachelard..* Montreal: Bellarmin, 1971.
Peyrou, Catherine, et al. *Bachelard: Colloque de Cérisy.* Paris: Union Generale d'"Editions, 1974.
Pire, Francois. *De l'imagination poétique dans l'oeuvre de Gaston Bachelard.* Paris: Corti, 1967.
Préclaire, Madeleine. *Une Poétique de l'homme, Essai sur l'imagination d'àpres l'oeuvre de Gaston Bachelard.* Montreal: Bellarmin, 1971.
Quillet, Pierre. *Bachelard.* Paris: Seghers, 1964.
Roy, Jean-Pierre. *Bachelard, ou le concept contre l'image.* Montreal: Presses de Univ. de Montréal, 1977.
Therrien, Vincent. *La Révolution de Gaston Bachelard en critique littéraire, ses fondements, ses techniques, sa portée, Du nouvel esprit scientifique à un nouvel esprit littéraire.* Paris: Klincksieck, 1970.

C. Articles about Bachelard

Bellemin-Nöel, Jean. "Bachelard ou le complexe de Tiresias." *Critique,* no. 270 (Nov. 1969), pp. 935-50.
Bernard, Michel-Georges. "L'Imagination parlée." *L'Arc,* no. 40 (1970), pp. 82-89.
Catesson, Jean. "Bachelard et les fondements de l'esthétique." *Critique,* 200 (Jan. 1964), pp. 45-51.
Christofides, C. G. "Gaston Bachelard and the Imagination of Matter." *Revue internationale de philosophie,* 66 (1963), 477-91.
_____. "Bachelard's Aesthetics." *Journal of Aesthetics and Art Criticism,* 20 (1962), 263-71.
Dagognet, Francois. "Gaston Bachelard, philosophe de l'imagination." *Revue internationale de philosophie,* 51 (1960), 32-42.
Dufrenne, Mikel. "Gaston Bachelard et la poésie de l'imagination." *Les Etudes philosophiques,* 4 (1963), 395-408.
Durand, Gilbert. "Psychanalyse de la neige." *Mercure de France,* 318 (1953), 615-39.
Elevitch, Bernard. "Gaston Bachelard: The Philosopher as Dreamer." *Dialogue,* vol. 7, no. 3 (1968), pp. 430-48.
Gaudin, Colette. "L'imagination et la rêverie: remarques sur la poétique de Gaston Bachelard." *Symposium,* 22 (1966), 207-25.
Grimsley, Ronald. "Two Philosophical Views of the Literary Imagination: Sartre and Bachelard." *Comparative Literature Studies,* vol. 8 (1971), pp. 42-57.
Higgonet, Margaret. "Bachelard and the Romantic Imagination." *Comparative Literature,* vol. 33, no. 1 (Winter 1981), pp. 18-37.
Jean, Raymond. "Lieu de la rêverie bachelardienne." *L'Arc,* no. 42 (1970), pp. 76-81.
Kaplan, Edward K. "Gaston Bachelard's Philosophy of Imagination: An Introduction." *Philosophy and Phenomenological Research,* 33, no. 2 (Sept. 1972), 1-24.
Lefèbve, Maurice-Jean. "De la science de profondeurs à la poésie des cimes." *Critique,* 200 (Jan. 1964), 28-40.
Oxenhandler, Neal. "Ontological Criticism in America and France." *The Modern Language Review,* 55 (1960), pp. 17-23.
Pariente, Jean-Claude. "Presence des images." *Critique,* 200 (Jan. 1964), pp. 3-27.
Poulet, Georges. "Gaston Bachelard et la conscience de soi." *Revue de metaphysique et de morale,* no. 1 (1965), pp. 1-26.

III. Collateral Readings

A. Books

Adorno, T. W. Horkheimer, Max. *Dialectic of Enlightenment.* Translated by John Cumming. New York: The Seabury Press, 1972.
Amis, Kingsley. *New Maps of Hell.* New York: Harcourt and Brace, 1960.
Attebery, Brian. *The Fantasy Tradition in American Literature: from Irving to Le Guin.* Bloomington: Indiana University Press, 1980.
Auden, W. H. *The Enchafed Flood: or The Romantic Iconography of the Sea.* New York: Random House, 1950.
Barnes, Hazel. *The Literature of Possibility, A Study in Humanistic Existentialism.* Lincoln: University of Nebraska Press, 1959.
Barrett, William. *The Illusion of Technique, A Search for Meaning in a Technological Civilization.* New York: Anchor Books, 1979.
Barthes, Roland. *Le Plaisir du texte.* Paris: Seuil, 1973.

Baudry, Jean Louis. "Freud et la création littéraire." In *Tel Quel, Théorie d'ensemble*. Dirigée par Philippe Sollers. Paris: Seuil, 1968, pp. 148-74.

Baxandall, Lee and Morawski, Stefan, eds. *Marx and Engels on Literature and Art, A Selection of Writings*. Milwaukee: Telos Press, 1973.

Bettelheim, Bruno. *The Uses of Enchantment, The Meaning and Importance of Fairy Tales*. New York: Vintage Books, 1965.

Bloch, Ernst. "The Meaning of Utopia" and "Utopia in Archetypes and Works of Art." In *Marxism and Art, Essays Classic and Contemporary*. Edited by Maynard Solomon. New York: Vintage Books, 1973. pp. 567-87.

_____. *A Philosophy of the Future*. Translated by John Cumming. New York: Herder and Herder, 1970.

Bodkin, Maud. *Archetypal Patterns in Poetry, Psychological Studies of Imagination*. Oxford: Oxford University Press, 1934.

Bonaparte, Princess Marie. *Edgar Poe, Etude psychanalytique*. Paris: DeNoël et Steel, 1933.

Booth, Wayne C. *The Rhetoric of Fiction*. Chicago: University of Chicago Press, 1961.

Bousquet, Jacques. *Les Thèmes du rêve dans la littérature romantique (France, Angleterre, Allegmagne), Essai sur la naissance et évolution des images*. Paris: Didier, 1964.

Camus, Albert. *Le Mythe de Sisyphe, Essai sur l'absurde*. Paris: Gallimard, 1942.

Carrouges, Michel. *Andre Bréton et les donnees fondamentales du surrealisme*. Paris: Gallimard, 1950.

Charles, Michel. *Rhétorique de la lecture*. Paris: Seuil, 1977.

Cirlot, J. E. *A Dictionary of Symbols*. Translated by Jack Sage. New York: Philosophical Library, 1962.

Cohn, Dorrit. *Transparent Minds, Narrative Modes for Presenting Consciousness in Literature*. Princeton: Princeton University Press, 1978.

Dallenbach, Lucien. *Le Récit spéculaire: Essai sur la mise en abîme*. Paris: Seuil, 1977.

de Man, Paul. "Modern Poetics." In *The Princeton Encyclopedia of Poetry and Poetics*. Edited by Alex Preminger. Princeton: Princeton University Press, 1972.

Diskin, Lahna. "Bradbury on Children." In *Ray Bradbury*. Writers of the Twenty-First Century Series. Edited by Martin Harry Greenberg and Joseph D. Olander. New York: Taplinger Pub., 1980, pp. 127-55.

Dufrenne, Mikel. *The Phenomenology of Aesthetic Experience*. Translated by E. S. Casey, et al. Evanston: Northwestern University Press, 1973.

Durand, Gilbert. *L'Imagination symbolique*. Deuxième ed. Paris: Presses Univ. de France, 1968.

Elliott, Robert C. *The Shape of Utopia*. Chicago: Chicago University Press, 1970.

Fischer, Ernst. *The Necessity of Art, A Marxist Approach*. Translated by Anna Bostock. Baltimore: Penguin Books, 1963.

Fordham, Frieda. *An Introduction to Jung's Psychology*. Baltimore: Penguin Books, 1953.

Freud, Sigmund. "The Acquisition of Power over Fire." In *Character and Culture*. Edited by Philip Rieff. Translated by Joan Riviere. New York: Collier Books, 1973, pp. 294-300.

_____. *Die Traumdeutung*. Frankfurt: S. Fischer Verlag, 1942.

_____. "Family Romances." In *The Sexual Enlightenment of Children*. Edited by Philip Rieff. Translated by James Strachey. New York: Collier Books, 1963, pp. 41-45.

Frey-Rohn, Liliane. *From Freud to Jung, A Comparative Study of the Unconscious*. Translated by Fred E. Engreen and Evelyn K. Engreen. New York: Dell Publishing Co., 1976.

Frye, Northrop. Preface to *The Psychoanalysis of Fire*. Translated by Alan C. M. Ross. Boston: Beacon Press, 1968, pp. v-viii.

_____. *The Anatomy of Criticism: Four Essays*. Princeton: Princeton University Press, 1957.

_____. *Fables of Identity, Studies in Poetic Mythology*. New York: Harcourt, Brace and World, 1963.

_____. *The Secular Scripture, A Study of the Structure of Romance.* Cambridge: Harvard University Press, 1976.

Gadamer, Hans-Georg. *Philosophical Hermeneutics.* Edited and translated by David E. Linge. Berkeley: University of California Press, 1976.

_____. *Truth and Method.* Translated by Garrett Barden and John Cumming. London: Sheed and Ward, 1975.

Gerber, Richard. *Utopian Fantasy, A Study of English Utopian Fiction Since the End of the Nineteenth Century.* New York: McGraw-Hill, 1973.

Gunn, James, *Alternate Worlds: The Illustrated History of Science Fiction.* New York: A and W Visual Library, 1975.

Hardison, O. B. Jr., ed. *The Quest for Imagination.* Cleveland: Case Western Reserve University Press, 1975.

Hartman, Geoffrey H. *The Fate of Reading and Other Essays.* Chicago: Chicago University Press, 1975.

Heidegger, Martin. *Poetry, Language, Thought.* Translated by Albert Hofstadter. New York: Harper and Row, 1971.

Hillegas, Mark R. *The Future as Nightmare, H. G. Wells and the Anti-Utopians.* New York: Oxford University Press, 1967.

Hirsch, E. D. Jr. *Validity in Interpretation.* New Haven: Yale University Press, 1967.

Hoffman, Daniel. *Poe, Poe, Poe, Poe, Poe, Poe, Poe.* New York: Avon Books, 1972.

Holland, Norman N. *The Dynamics of Literary Response.* New York: W. W. Norton and Co., 1975.

_____. *Poems in Persons: An Introduction to the Psychoanalysis of Literature.* New York: W. W. Norton and Co., 1973.

Hoy, David Couzens. *The Critical Circle, Literature, History, and Philosophical Hermeneutics.* Berkeley: University of California Press, 1978.

Ingarden, Roman. *The Cognition of the Literary Work of Art.* Translated by Ruth Ann Crowley and Kenneth R. Olson. Evanston: Northwestern University Press, 1973.

_____. *The Literary Work of Art, An Investigation on the Borderline of Ontology, Logic, and Theory of Literature.* Translated by George C. Grabowicz. Evanston: Northwestern University Press, 1973.

Irwin, W. R. *The Game of the Impossible, A Rhetoric of Fantasy.* Urbana: University of Illinois Press, 1976.

Iser, Wolfgang. *The Act of Reading, A Theory of Aesthetic Response.* Baltimore: Johns Hopkins University Press, 1978.

_____. *The Implied Reader, Patterns in Communication in Prose Fiction from Bunyan to Beckett.* Baltimore: Johns Hopkins University Press, 1974.

_____. "Indeterminacy and the Reader's Response in Prose Fiction." In *Aspects of Narrative, English Institute Essays.* Edited by J. Hillis Miller. New York: Columbia University Press, 1971, pp. 1-45.

Jacobi, Jolande. *Complex/Archetype/Symbol in the Psychology of C. G. Jung.* Translated by Ralph Manheim. New York: Pantheon Books, 1959.

_____. *The Psychology of Jung, An Introduction with Illustrations.* Translated by Ralph Manheim. New Haven: Yale University Press, 1973.

Jacobi, Mario. "The Analytical Psychology of C. G. Jung and the Problem of Literary Evaluation." In *Problems of Literary Evaluation: Yearbook of Comparative Criticism, Vol. II.* Edited by Joseph Strelka. University Park: Penn State Press, 1971.

Jameson, Frederic. *Marxism and Form, Twentieth-Century Dialectical Theories of Literature.* Princeton: Princeton University Press, 1971.

Jung, C. G. *Four Archetypes: Mother/Rebirth/Spirit/Trickster.* Translated by R. F. C. Hull. Princeton: Princeton University Press, 1969.

_____. "The Psychology of the Child Archetype." In *Essays on a Science of Mythology, The Myth of the Divine Child and the Mysteries of Eleusis*. Translated by R. F. C. Hull, Princeton: Princeton: Princeton University Press, 1963, pp. 70-100.

_____. *Psychological Types*. Translated by H. G. Baynes, revised by R. F. C. Hull. London: Routledge and Kegan Paul, 1971.

_____. "Relations Between the Ego and the Unconscious." In *The Portable Jung*. Edited by Joseph Campbell. Translated by R. F. C. Hull. New York: Viking Press, 1971, pp. 70-138.

_____. *The Spirit in Man, Art, and Literature*. Translated by R. F. C. Hull. Princeton: Princeton University Press, 1971.

Kaelin, Eugene, *An Existentialist Aesthetic*. Milwaukee: University of Wisconsin Press, 1966.

Kern, Edith. *Existential Thought and Fictional Technique: Kierkegaard, Sartre, Beckett*. New Haven: Yale University Press, 1970.

Ketterer, David. *New Worlds for Old, The Apocalyptic Imagination, Science Fiction, and American Literature*. New York: Avon Books, 1974.

Kolakowski, Leszek. "The Psychoanalytic Theory of Culture." In *Psychological Man*. Edited by Robert Boyers. New York: Harper and Row, 1975, pp. 27-56.

LaPlanche, Jean and J. B. Pontalis. *Vocabulaire de la psychanalyse*. Paris: Presses Univ. de France, 1967.

Lasch, Christopher. *The Culture of Narcissism, American Life in an Age of Diminishing Expectations*. New York: Warner Books, 1979.

Lauer, Quentin. *Phenomenology: Its Genesis and Prospect*. New York: Harper and Row, 1965.

Lawall, Sarah N. *Critics of Consciousness, The Existential Structures of Literature*. Cambridge: Harvard University Press, 1968.

Lawler, Donald L., ed. *Approaches to Science Fiction*. Boston: Houghton Mifflin, 1978.

LeGuin, Ursula K. *The Language of the Night, Essays in Fantasy and Science Fiction*. Edited with introduction by Susan Wood. New York: G. P. Putnam's Sons, 1979.

Lesser, Simon O. *Fiction and the Unconscious*. New York: Vintage, 1957

Lukacs, Georg. *Writer and Critic and Other Essays*. Translated and edited by Arthur D. Kahn. New York: Grosset and Dunlap, 1971.

Luthi, Max. *Once Upon a Time, On the Nature of Fairy Tales*. Translated by Chadeayne and Paul Gottwald. Bloomington: Indiana University Press, 1976.

Magliola, Robert R. *Phenomenology and Literature: An Introduction*. West Lafayette: Purdue University Press, 1977.

Manlove, C. N. *Modern Fantasy: Five Studies*. London: Cambridge University Press, 1975.

Marcuse, Herbert. *Eros and Civilization, A Philosophical Inquiry into Freud*. New York: Vintage, 1962.

_____. *One-Dimensional Man, Studies in the Ideology of Advanced Industrial Society*. Boston: Beacon Press, 1964.

Marin, Louis, *Utopiques: Jeux d'espaces*. (Paris: Minuit, 1973).

Matthews, J. H, *Toward the Poetics of Surrealism*. Syracuse: Syracuse University Press, 1976.

Merleau-Ponty, Maurice. *Signs*. Translated by Richard C. McCleary. Evanston: Northwestern University Press, 1964.

_____. *The Structure of Behavior*. Translated by Alden Fisher. Boston: Beacon Press, 1963.

Miller, J. Hillis. "The Geneva School: The Criticism of Marcel Raymond, Albert Beguin, Georges Poulet, Jean Rousset, Jean Pierre Richard, and Jean Starobinski." In *Modern French Criticism*. Edited by John K. Simon. Chicago: Chicago University Press, 1972, pp. 277-310.

Minkowski, Eugene. *Vers une cosmologie*. Paris: Aubier, 1936.

Neumann, Erich. *The Origins and History of Consciousness*. Translated by R. F. C. Hull. Princeton University Press, 1954.

Poe, Edgar Allan. *Complete Tales and Poems*. New York: Vintage Books, 1975.

_____. "The Philosophy of Composition." In *American Poetic Theory.* Edited by George Perkins. New York: Holt, Rinehart and Winston, 1972, pp. 27-38.

Philipson, Morris. *Outline of Jungian Aesthetics.* Evanston: Northwestern University Press, 1963.

Pierce, Hazel. "Ray Bradbury and the Gothic Tradition." In *Ray Bradbury.* Writers of the Twenty-First Century Series. Edited by Martin Harry Greenberg and Joseph D. Olander. New York: Taplinger Pub. Co., 1980, pp. 165-85.

Poulet, Georges. *Etudes sur le temps humain.* Paris: Plon, 1956.

_____. *La conscience critique.* Paris: Corti, 1971.

Rabkin, Eric S. *The Fantastic in Literature.* Princeton: Princeton University Press, 1976.

_____, ed. *Fantastic Worlds: Myths, Tales, and Stories.* New York: Oxford University Press, 1979.

_____. *Narrative Suspense.* Ann Arbor: University of Michigan Press, 1973.

_____. "To Fairyland by Rocket: Bradbury's *The Martian Chronicles.*" In *Ray Bradbury: Writers of the Twenty-First Century Series.* Edited by Martin Harry Greenberg and Joseph D. Olander. New York: Taplinger Pub. Co., 1980, pp. 110-26.

_____. *Arthur C. Clarke.* Starmont Reader's Guides, No. 1. Mercer Island: Starmont House, 1980.

Raymond, Marcel. *Romantisme et rêverie.* Paris: Corti, 1978.

Sachs, Hans. "A Digression into Movie-Land." In his *The Creative Unconscious, Studies in the Psychoanalysis of Art.* Cambridge, Mass.: Sci-Art Pub., 1942, pp. 178-89.

Saraiva, Maria Manuela. *L'Imagination selon Husserl.* Le Haye: Martinus Nijhoff, 1970.

Sartre, Jean-Paul. *Esquisse d'une theorie des émotions.* Paris: Herman, 1965. *L'Imaginaire.* Paris: Gallimard, 1940. *L'Imagination.* 6th ed. Paris: Presses University de France, 1965.

Scholes, Robert and Kellogg, Robert. *The Nature of Narrative.* New York: Oxford University Press, 1966.

Scholes, Robert and Rabkin, Eric S. *Science Fiction: History, Science, Vision.* New York: Oxford University Press, 1977.

Scholes, Robert; Rabkin, Eric S., and Slusser, George E., eds. *Bridges to Fantasy.* Carbondale: Southern Illinois University Press, 1982.

Shklovsky, Victor. "Art as Technique." In *Russian Formalist Criticism: Four Essays.* Translated by Lee T. Lemon and Marion J. Reis. Lincoln: University of Nebraska Press, 1965, pp. 3-24.

Slochower, Harry. *Mythopoesis, Mythic Patterns in the Literary Classics.* Detroit: Wayne State University Press, 1970.

Solomon, Maynard, ed. *Marxism and Art, Essays Classic and Contemporary.* New York: Vintage Books, 1973.

Stacy, Robert H. *Defamiliarization in Language and Literature.* Syracuse: Syracuse University Press, 1977.

Suvin, Darko, *Metamorphoses of Science Fiction, On the Poetics and History of a Literary Genre.* New Haven: Yale University Press, 1979.

Tillich, Paul. "Critique and Justification of Utopia." In *Utopias and Utopian Thought, A Timely Appraisal.* Edited by Frank E. Manuel. Boston: Beacon Press, 1965, pp. 296-309.

Todorov, Tzvetan. *The Fantastic, A Structural Approach to a Literary Genre.* Translated by Richard Howard. Forward by Robert Scholes. Ithaca: Cornell University Press, 1975.

Tolkien, J. R. R. "On Fairy-Stories." In *The Tolkien Reader.* New York: Ballantine Books, 1966, pp. 3-73.

Tompkins, Jane P., ed. *Reader-Response Criticism: from Formalism to Post-Structuralism.* Baltimore: Johns Hopkins University Press, 1980.

Tuzet, Helene. *Le Cosmos et l'imagination.* Paris: Corti, 1965.

Watt, Donald. "Burning Bright, *Fahrenheit 451* as a Symbolic Dystopia." In *Ray Bradbury.* Writers of the Twenty-First Century Series. Edited by Martin Harry Greenberg and Joseph D. Olander. New York: Taplinger Pub. Co., 1980, pp. 195-213.

B. Articles

Allen, Jeffner. "A Husserlian Phenomenology of the Child." *Journal of Phenomenological Psychology,* vol. 6, no. 2 (Spring 1976), pp. 169-80.

Dällenbach, Lucien. "Reflexivity and Reading." *New Literary History,* vol. 11, no. 3 (Spring 1980), pp. 435-49.

De Maria, Robert Jr. "The Ideal Reader: A Critical Fiction." *PMLA,* 93 (1978), 463-74.

Elkins, Charles and Suvin, Darko. "Preliminary Reflections on Teaching Science Fiction Critically." *Science Fiction Studies,* vol. 6, no. 19 (1979), pp. 263-70.

Fredericks, S. C. "Problems of Fantasy." *Science Fiction Studies,* 5 (1978), pp. 33-44.

Huntington, John. "Utopian and Anti-Utopian Logic: H. G. Wells and his Successors," *Science Fiction Studies,* vol. 9, part 2, no. 27 (July 1982), pp. 122-46.

Iser, Wolfgang. "The Current Situation of Literary Theory: Key Concepts and the Imaginary." *New Literary History,* vol. 11, no. 1 (Autumn 1979), pp. 1-20.

Jauss, Hans Robert. "Levels of Identification of Hero and Audience." *New Literary History,* vol. 5, no. 2 (Winter 1974), pp. 284-317.

Kuenzli, Rudolf E. "Interview with Wolfgang Iser." *Diacritics,* vol. 10, no. 2 (June 1980), pp. 57-74.

LaPlanche, Jean and Pontalis, J. B. "Fantasme originaire, fantasme de origines, origine du fantasme." *Les Temps modernes,* 19 (1964), 1833-68.

Mailloux, Stephen. "Reader-Response Criticism?" *Genre,* vol. 5, no. 3 (Fall 1977), pp. 423-27.

Morrissey, Robert. "Vers un topos littéraire. la préhistoire de la rêverie." *Modern Philology,* vol. 77, no. 3 (Feb. 1980), pp. 261-90.

Poulet, Georges. "Phenomenology of Reading." *New Literary History,* 1 (1969), 53-68.

Ray, William. "Recognizing Recognition: The Intra-Textual and Extra-Textual Critical Persona." *Diacritics,* vol. 7, no. 4 (Winter, 1977), pp. 20-33.

Scholes, Robert. "Cognition and the Implied Reader." *Diacritics,* vol. 5, no. 3 (Fall 1975), pp. 13-15.

Wilson, W. Daniel. "Readers in Texts." *PMLA* 96/5 (Oct. 1981), pp. 848-63.

Index